The Western church is struggling deeply in a time of real decline and growing apathy toward the Christian tradition. In this thoughtful and provocative book, Craig begins to pave the way forward for how we can join Jesus in seeking and saving the lost in these complex and challenging times.

Jon Tyson, author, *Beautiful Resistance*; pastor,
Church of the City, New York

Craig has a passion for helping people find faith in Jesus Christ. Through his outstanding leadership of Alpha USA I have experienced his commitment to unity across the church and his infectious reliance on the Holy Spirit. I am so pleased that he has produced this resource on evangelism for leaders.

Nicky Gumbel, pioneer of The Alpha Course

We need a revival: personally, in our churches, in our communities, and in the nation. And we need to be okay trying new things, talking less, listening more, asking better questions, and creating space for real, deep spiritual renewal to happen over time. I recommend this book to any church leader looking to rethink the way their communities live and share good news. And I want my college students to get a hold of this book that speaks their language and understands their experience. Pay attention to what Craig says!

Miriam Swanson, Global Student Mission; leader, Fusion Movement

The fork in culture between followers of Jesus and the unchurched is widening. This calls not for alarm or fear, nor should we dig in our heels to continue using "tried and true" methods that may have worked in a different cultural moment in the past. Craig's book offers seven ways to revive evangelism in an effective way today, and I think he is on to something. He writes with a hopeful and encouraging perspective and offers significant research and insights to reach unchurched Millennials and those in Gen Z. I commend this timely book!

Ed Stetzer, Wheaton College

Craig writes as someone who understands the challenges we have faced and the emotional f.... ed. In *How to Revive Evangelism* ᵒach that will inspire you to dr

an Inside Job;
TMS Global

This book by my friend Craig is a breath of fresh air in the somewhat stale and formulaic genre of writing on evangelism. Craig is an inspiring leader and a good exemplar of these ideas, and his book deserves a wide audience.

Alan Hirsch, award-winning author and
founder, Movement Leaders Collective
and Forge Missional Training Network

Evangelism is a great challenge in these "post everything" days. Many have retreated, discouraged, from the front lines, sure that there's nothing to be done. My friend Craig lays out seven practical, strategic changes we can and should make in our approach to evangelism. This isn't one more "sure-fire program" but rather an inspirational journey that can help us become more effective. Be renewed as you read and rediscover what you were made for!

Kevin Palau, president, Luis Palau Association

Craig Springer's new book equips us in a way of evangelism which is real, authentic, holistic, transformative, and refreshing. If you read it, you will walk away empowered and excited to evangelize again.

Sam Chan, author, *Evangelism in a Skeptical World*;
public speaker for City Bible Forum, Australia

I'm thrilled for Craig's new book! This is a deeply challenging yet inspirational, hope-filled clarion call for the church.

Keri Ladouceur, pastor, Community Christian
Church; founder, New Ground Network

A timely reminder that people are looking to belong before they believe. Craig Springer has given the Church a practical and prophetic gift in his fabulous new book.

Jeanne Stevens, founding lead pastor,
Soul City Church, Chicago

Get ready to be launched into deeper waters and more effective evangelism.

Dr. Stacy Spencer, senior pastor, New
Direction Church, Memphis

How to
Revive
Evangelism

7 Vital Shifts in How
We Share Our Faith

Craig Springer

ZONDERVAN
REFLECTIVE

ZONDERVAN REFLECTIVE

How to Revive Evangelism
Copyright © 2021 by Alpha USA

ISBN 978-0-310-11469-7 (softcover)

ISBN 978-0-310-11472-7 (audio)

ISBN 978-0-310-11470-3 (ebook)

Requests for information should be addressed to:
Zondervan, *3900 Sparks Dr. SE, Grand Rapids, Michigan 49546*

Published in association with The Christopher Ferebee Agency, www .christopherferebee.com.

Cover design: LUCAS Art and Design
Interior typesetting: Kait Lamphere

Printed in the United States of America

20 21 22 23 24 25 26 27 28 /LSC/ 12 11 10 9 8 7 6 5 4 3 2 1

Contents

Foreword

By David Kinnaman

First things first. I desperately want to see the Church more faithful and fruitful today. What could be more important than to see people's hearts come alive to Jesus? And as you'll see in this book, that's a question we should be asking ourselves not only for non-believers but also for *Christians*, too.

Yet, so much stands in the way of this mission. Especially today. Major secularizing forces which have been long at work—and the crazy amount of disruption brought on by the coronavirus pandemic—are only going to make the task of spiritual renewal more difficult.

The best way I know how to contribute to this cause is to generate research-based analysis and insights to help Christian leaders gain a clear picture of what's really happening in hearts and minds. That's why, I believe, God has called me to lead Barna Group. We often describe our vision as derived from 1 Chronicles 12:32—to help understand the times and know what to do.

For that reason, this book, *How to Revive Evangelism*, blows me away: it's firmly anchored to reality and pursues a hopeful vision of real-life evangelism. My friend Craig Springer isn't just making up ideas or guessing his way to applications. In fact, some years ago, as he first started to lead Alpha US, he asked our team at Barna to conduct a major research project on the state of evangelism in the US. He wanted to grasp the current contours of ministry. That project resulted in a comprehensive report called *Reviving Evangelism* (which you can helpfully read alongside this book, if you choose).

And now, in Craig's book you'll see up close how a remarkable, passionate leader has leveraged research insights and is wrestling them to the ground for today's context, for real-world impact. In addition, this book draws from applications that have been tried and true, hard-earned through many decades of ministry: Craig planted a church in the Czech Republic; he's served at large churches here in the US.; he's been hearing from pastors and leaders through his role leading Alpha US. *How to Revive Evangelism* pulls from all these sources to create a beautiful tapestry of faithful insights. What a listener and learner Craig shows himself to be!

That is rare.

Far too many leaders plan ministry and strategy for a world as it used to be or as they wish it were, not for the world as it actually is. I believe this book—and the seven shifts that Craig proposes—are well tuned to the context we actually have. Together, we've done the homework;

as you read this practical, inspiring book, you'll see that richly displayed.

I expect that many who read this book will be familiar with Alpha or even running Alpha. For those who are, I believe the seven shifts Craig describes will help you to articulate and embody the most transformative parts of Alpha in your church community. In other words, I anticipate this book will become something of a training guide and manifesto for what makes Alpha work so well.

For readers who are *unfamiliar* with Alpha, you will come across many descriptions and stories of Alpha in these pages. I think you should know that Alpha doesn't have anything to sell to churches or Christian leaders. That's unique. It's not a club you join, or a product or program. There's no subscription fee or cost. It's just a way of thinking about and living out the evangelism call, which I think leaders can learn a lot from. Craig's enthusiasm for Alpha should not dampen the power of the transferable principles he's learned, whether you choose to run Alpha or not.

I am encouraging you, then, dear reader, not simply to take benefit from Barna's research and Craig's applications but to also consider how to become a student of culture and a learner yourself. How could you come to apply rigor, research, self-evaluation, and the sacred art of listening to others whom you are trying to reach?

These habits are themselves an important way to revive evangelism. When I worked on the book *unChristian*—which showed the brutal reality of the negative perceptions of young non-Christians toward Christianity (the world as it is)—I found that many Christians resisted the findings. They critiqued the methodology. They criticized the non-Christians (*Their minds are blinded by Satan, right? How could they even know what to think?*). They said my coauthor, Gabe Lyons, and I were off our rockers. Sure, the research has limitations (as all research does) and the authors were imperfect messengers. Still, the critics did almost everything but listen to and learn, to really hear what young people were saying about the Church and what that might mean for a faithful way forward.

Yet, to revive evangelism in our time—to help people truly be set free in Jesus—we need to be learners and listeners. The pages of Scripture are filled with the lofty aspiration that we should have ears to hear and eyes to see.

Barna's work and Craig's insights strongly suggest new approaches to evangelism and discipleship are needed. This particular book is a helpful and practical playbook to a new way of evangelism, deeply rooted in the ancient truths of Scripture, for our oncoming era.

Let those who have ears, listen!

David Kinnaman is president of the Barna Group, author of *You Lost Me*, *Good Faith*, and *Faith for Exiles*, and coauthor of *unChristian*. He lives in Ventura, California.

It's Not Working Anymore

What do ugly Christmas sweaters, bacon-wrapped dates, the next *Star Wars* movie, smoked ribs, meatless *Impossible* burgers, new hairdos, and Taylor Swift's new song all have in common?

I saw these images during six seconds of scrolling through Instagram this morning. That's what people are sharing, from the popular to the unbelievable, from what moves us to what amazes us. We share what we love and experience (or whatever public "dumpster-fire" seems to be burning at the moment)—it's hard-wired into our DNA to want to share with others. Many of us can't even refrain from spilling the movie spoilers. I'm guessing you've heard a preacher (or three, or thirteen) use this analogy when it comes to sharing our faith:

We love Jesus, he's changed our lives—so just like we tell people about that Wagyu beef burger, new romantic friend, or our favorite kale salad surprise (maybe not that one), so too should we share about Jesus!

And why wouldn't we want to share about Jesus, this person who has changed everything for us? Why wouldn't we talk to others about the Christian faith, the foundation we have dedicated ourselves to learning more about, the movement that transformed our lives?

But, overwhelmingly, we're simply not sharing our faith anymore. It's the one area where this impulse to talk about the good stuff seems to be fading, and fast.

In the US especially, the instinct to evangelize is eroding.

No matter how much our walk with Jesus has impacted our lives, many of us simply aren't talking about it—not to our families, not to our friends, and not within our communities. The data shows this on a number of levels, and the conclusive nature of the findings should be setting off alarm bells everywhere.

Sharing My Faith . . . Is Wrong

Forty-seven percent of Millennial Christians believe sharing their faith with others is wrong.[1]

Let that sink in.

That's nearly one-half of all young Christians from their early 20s to late 30s, nearly two decades worth of believers, who think sharing their faith is fundamentally wrong. They're not saying it's undesirable. They're not saying it's too difficult or that they're not sure what words to use to communicate their faith to others.

They're actually saying they believe it's wrong to share their faith.

How can we pass on the baton of faithfulness and fulfill the Great Commission, how can we transfer a passion for sharing our faith, when nearly half of an entire generation is saying, "It's not that I don't want to share my faith—it's wrong for me to do it"?

When you look at the other generations, though—the GenXers, the Boomers, and the Elders—the data shows their lack of interaction with the broader culture poses its own set of problems. On the whole, half of the Christians in the United States have just two spiritual conversations per year[2] or fewer. We're talking about basic spiritual conversations—not intense dialogues on the depth and breadth of the substitutionary atonement or pre-tribulation end times theology. And 38 percent of adult Christians in the United States don't have a single non-Christian friend or family member.[3] Many who are older than Millennials have drifted into an impenetrable Christian bubble, largely unengaged with the culture and communities around us.

By 2050, if the current trends continue unaltered, 35 million youth[4] raised in families that call themselves Christians will say that they are not. Church attendance is in decline in every generation,[5] and there is hardly a net neutral impact from church planting each year when we account for the number of churches officially closing.[6]

That's a massive hemorrhage at a time when we are trying to grow our legacy of faith for the future and fulfill the Great Commission. And, there's precious little evidence to show that new people are darkening the doors of our churches at any kind of substantial, widespread rate.

It would be relatively easy, given the statistics, to sit back and blame Millennials for the church's attendance and growth problems. Right? After all, most segments of society have figured out a way to pin the blame for all sorts of things on the Millennials. "Millennials killed bookstores, Millennials killed the breakfast cereal fad, Millennials killed the housing market, Millennials killed cable TV, Millennials even killed marriage!" It's *obviously* the device-addicted, avocado-toast eating, participation-trophy earning, self-righteous, entitled generation wanting to live their best life now without working for it. We might overlay the evangelism problem and the decline with each consecutive generation, look at the Millennial stats, and land in a place of Millennial shaming and blaming. Many go further and view Millennials as the generation who no longer believes Jesus is *the* way to salvation.

Millennials, in many people's minds, should bear the lion's share of the blame for the decline of the church in Western society.

Before we go further, though, who raised them? Who passed out the participation trophies, handed down whatever attitudes and beliefs they have, or provided evangelism strategies Millennial Christians find untenable?

We don't need to play the blame game though. We just

need to get to the bottom of this challenge and change whatever we can. Fortunately, there are nuggets of information in our studies that lead us to believe Millennials, and specifically Millennial Christians, actually hold the key to the future growth of the church.

That's right.

Millennials, in many ways, have cracked the code.

One of the key statistics not often mentioned in the doom-and-gloom reports about the state of Millennial Christians is this: 94 percent of Millennial Christians think the best thing that could ever happen to someone is for them to come to know Jesus.[7] What an incredible statement! And that is generally in line with each prior generation of Christian adults.

What does this tell us? What's happening among Millennial Christians is not necessarily a lack of belief or a lack of desire for others to know Christ, nor is it a lack of evangelistic self-confidence. After all, 73 percent of Millennial Christians believe they are equipped and gifted at sharing their faith with others,[8] a higher percentage than any prior generation.[9] And the Millennial generation overall is having more spiritual conversations than any other generation.[10] We even discovered in the data that Millennial non-Christians are twice as likely to express personal interest in Christianity than older non-Christians.[11] Wow. There is hunger, there is desire, and there is a willingness to explore faith. Finally, Millennial Christians have more non-Christian friends outside the church than any prior generation. Unlike most other generational cohorts, Millennials are connected and in touch, not stuck in the bubble.

What if Millennial Christians are not disengaging from evangelism because their faith is wavering but because they understand the static characteristics of our evangelistic approaches are not as effective in today's dynamic culture?

What if our methodologies of evangelism, designed to work during the past fifty years or so, are something like a cassette tape that we ask Millennials to play when what they're really looking for is a Spotify playlist?

What if we have designed ways of communicating for a perceived Christianized culture in "Jerusalem" when the time we are living in now more closely resembles secular "Babylon"?[12]

What if Millennial Christians have a better understanding of the polarized, inflamed, *disagreement-equals-judgment* culture our world has devolved into and are trying to find other ways to navigate and influence it besides simply proclaiming the truth indiscriminately?

Keeping in mind all the data, our main question shouldn't center around what's wrong with Millennials, how they are to blame for the current state of the church, or where their faith has gone.

Our primary question should be, "What do Millennial Christians know that we can all learn from to reach our world for Jesus?"

The "Post-Everything" Era

Maybe you have felt the challenges, too, even if you're not a Millennial. Maybe you've had that creeping sense of guilt when you're starting a friendship with someone simply so you can make an inroad for evangelism. Maybe you've been in a situation in which you're sharing the gospel but realize the person you're talking to has some major, tangible barriers to Jesus in their life preventing them from moving forward. Maybe you have friends who have felt increasingly judged by the church and are unwilling to ever attend. You're not even sure where to begin sharing the good news with them when their only exposure has left them feeling anxious, beaten down, or pushed away.

Culture has shifted. We are entering a new epoch. It is possible, according to a recent tweet from author and pastor Tim Keller, that this is the first time in the history of the church where we've had to learn how to navigate a post-Christian culture. Historically, the church has almost always operated in pre-Christian or even Christian contexts. But now, especially in Westernized countries, generations are growing up in a post-Christian environment, where the memory of past spiritual relevance has faded and dulled the impact of faith. Generations are now growing up inoculated against the impact of Christ in our communities. Add to this the moral controversies swirling around and within our Christian churches and it's no wonder culture is sprinting in the opposite direction.

Tectonic shifts are occurring which press us toward what author, podcaster, and pastor John Mark Comer calls a "post-everything" era. The following are four major "posts" that have brought our culture to the place it is today—creating a new, virtually unexplored world regarding Christian life and evangelism.

Post-Christian

This movement into a post-Christian culture can be seen in how one fundamental question has changed. We used to ask each other, "Where do you go to church?" But that question has morphed into something entirely different. Now the more common question in our culture is, "Why would you go to church?"

At a recent Alpha training event, a senior pastor insisted over and over that this post-Christian culture we were talking about just wasn't his reality. "People still want to come to church," he explained. "We just need to try a little harder."

But later, the pastor's younger team member pulled one of us aside. "We are definitely in a post-Christian culture—it's just not in our senior pastor's field of vision. He's navigating thousands of Boomers, but there's a younger generation I'm seeing who are unsettled and asking a lot of questions and unwilling to show up to what we've created."

Most of us in the West have gone from living in a Christian culture to a post-Christian culture. Some of us just haven't recognized it yet.

Post-Family

We have transitioned from a culture where family stability and cohesion is assumed to the opposite: Many people in our culture do not have a sense of connection with an intimate family unit. The percentage of children living with two parents in their first marriage dropped 27 percent from 1960 to 2014 (from 73 percent to 46 percent).

And the number of children living with a single parent has nearly tripled during that time.[13]

Some of this has to do with divorce rates and some of it has to do with mobility, but much of this change can be traced back to the pace of life, our overcommitment to activities, and the creep of work into every corner of our lives.

Even something as simple as the family dinner is increasingly extinct, gradually rubbed out of existence by carpools that need to go in five different directions, sports schedules, entertainment media distraction, and households where parents work all day.

The idea of sitting around the table and having a meaningful conversation with our family is, for most people in our culture, a thing of the past. We can all have an opinion online (and we certainly aren't afraid to use it!), but the opportunities to meet in person and respectfully exchange ideas and opinions are few and far between. This profound loss begins with the family and extends into broader social circles.

Because of this relatively new loss of family structure, there's a longing, a craving, especially in the Millennial generation and younger, to connect on deep levels with others.

Post-Technology

The third change Comer points out begins with the birth of the iPhone and the way it has transformed how we understand connection. This began with easier texting and moved from there into "following" or "friending" on Facebook, Twitter, and Instagram.

Now, I'm not a social media or technology Luddite, but it's so important to realize many people in today's generation look at their compiled list of social media "friends" and think, *"Wow, I'm connected to so many people!"* The reality is that according to every major metric, we feel less meaningfully connected. "[S]tudies have linked the use of social media to depression, anxiety, poorer sleep quality, lower self-esteem, inattention, and hyperactivity—often in teens and adolescents."[14]

Technology hasn't only pulled us out of family conversations—it has pulled us out of almost every type of conversation we used to have. Recovering the art of dialogue and meaningful connection is one of the greatest challenges, and opportunities, presented to the church in this post-technology era.

Post-Super-Size

This last post- is a tricky one to talk about, because in some ways the megachurch is flourishing in America. I served within two significant mega-churches before I came to Alpha. My goal is not to deconstruct or blow up an architecture of church that God is clearly using in the twenty-first century.

But we also need to hold this in tension. There is a generation longing for a church experience where they aren't lost in the crowd, a church where the experience of its parishioners isn't limited to thousands of people in a huge venue watching a screen or solely stuck at home watching an impersonal screen online. Crafting anonymity used to be the goal in megachurch planning meetings; now the question is, "How can our large gatherings and our mega megaphone create more inroads for deep, personal connection?"

Many young Christian leaders who grew up among the megachurch movements are now dreaming of the church they want to plant, and they're often envisioning a smaller-scale, more intimate church, a community involved in the context of their city, one where they can know and be known.

They are looking for something connected, conversational —the kind of place where they can share the entirety of their life journey. They don't find enough value in just a weekly hit of quick hellos or on screen likes, and they realize surface-level spaces won't transform the next generation.

Perhaps that's one of the greatest challenges faced by large churches: How can we integrate this kind of community experience into the life of the megachurch? Without deconstructing the corporate gathering, where is the space in a larger church for people to journey together? Where are the spaces where people from the outside can feel like they belong and truly connect before they are willing to believe?

So, what do we do with this?

Throw up our hands in hopelessness?

Sing our worship songs louder so that we don't have to listen to culture's dissenting voice? Keep sharing our faith in the same manner with deteriorating results, while overall church attendance shrinks and the incoming generations retreat from our expressions of Christian faith?

Give up?

We don't have to lose hope, ignore the problem, or give up, because the church is uniquely positioned to fill all these unmet needs in this post-everything era.

- Our post-Christian culture is yearning for deep, meaningful dialogue about spiritual things.
- Our post-family culture is looking for a place where they can belong.
- Our post-technology culture is seeking out genuine interactions.
- Our post-super-size culture desires intimate communities.

The church, as the vehicle of the Holy Spirit, can fulfill these innate longings, but if we're going to do that in all our different contexts and communities, if we are going to find a way forward in this post-everything era, it will be through seven primary shifts in how we share our faith.

1. *We have to be hungry for more, not just hoping for many.*
2. *We have to engage in conversation, not just proclamation.*
3. *We have to create spaces of belonging, not just welcoming.*

4. *We must speak through experience, not just explanation.*
5. *Our concern must be with the fruitful, not just the factual.*
6. *Our efforts must involve we, not just me.*
7. *We need to build unity, not just uniformity.*

We can turn this situation around.

But Because You Say So

Let me be up front: This is not my attempt to share a shiny new program or a "secret sauce" for evangelism. The seven shifts I'm proposing are timely adjustments, all of which are strongly rooted in the timeless approach of Jesus. Each shift is crucial to re-engaging our culture.

Jesus shows us an old, new way. It doesn't always make sense to those of us ingrained in the current ways, but if we employ Jesus' approach, we'll begin to see a rising tide.

There's no better summary than when Jesus first called his disciples in Luke 5:1–11:

One day as Jesus was standing by the Lake of Gennesaret, the people were crowding around him and listening to the word of God. He saw at the water's edge two boats, left there by the fishermen, who were washing their nets. He got into one of the boats, the one belonging to Simon, and asked him to put out a little from shore. Then he sat down and taught the people from the boat.

When he had finished speaking, he said to Simon, "Put out into deep water, and let down the nets for a catch."

Simon answered, "Master, we've worked hard all night and haven't caught anything. But because you say so, I will let down the nets."

When they had done so, they caught such a large number of fish that their nets began to break. So they signaled their partners in the other boat to come and help them, and they came and filled both boats so full that they began to sink.

When Simon Peter saw this, he fell at Jesus' knees and said, "Go away from me, Lord; I am a sinful man!" For he and all his companions were astonished at the catch of fish they had taken, and so were James and John, the sons of Zebedee, Simon's partners.

Then Jesus said to Simon, "Don't be afraid; from now on you will fish for people." So they pulled their boats up on shore, left everything and followed him.

Can you imagine yourself in that moment? These disciples had been out fishing all night, hadn't caught a thing, and returned to shore to clean their nets, only to have their boats commandeered by a local construction worker rabbi. Then, at the end of his teaching, he's impudent enough to tell them, as they're cleaning up, where to go if they want to catch fish!

Think about that for a second. How do you respond when someone shows up in your area of expertise and starts making suggestions? I know I don't always accept that kind of "help" very gracefully. These fishermen knew that lake like the back of their hand. They knew the best time of day to fish, the best places to fish, and they knew that, sometimes, the fish just aren't there to catch. Sometimes you have to call it a day.

Besides their expertise, they were just plain worn out—exhausted after a long night of waiting. They were more than a little discouraged. I'd imagine they were ready to go home, recline with their feet up, and sip on some Galilean wine.

Enter Jesus.

He tells them now's the time to fish, and he tells them where to fish. The first half of Peter's response is where most of us relate. To be honest, I might have stopped there too.

"Master, we've worked hard all night and haven't caught anything."

Pause for a second.

Isn't that the place where many of us are when it comes to evangelism? Haven't most of us worked hard, analyzed the trends, tried to discover what's working for other people, and implemented those programs . . . only to get to the end of a long period of time and pull up empty or almost empty nets? I know I have. No wonder a certain kind of defeatism has begun to creep into our evangelism efforts. We've worked hard, we've worked smart, and we haven't seen results—at least not the results we've been praying for.

But have we tried the counterintuitive ways of Jesus

when it comes to evangelism? Have we looked at his interactions with people? Have we studied the reactions of those who were changed by him? Have we listened to his voice and cast our nets into a time and place that didn't quite make sense?

Because let's be honest—Jesus' recommendation to Peter and the other fishermen wasn't exactly in line with standard fishing practices.

Yet, almost inexplicably, Peter and the other fishermen listened to Jesus. Peter didn't stop to explain how tired they were or how they had tried everything. He simply said, "But because you say so, I will let down the nets."

But because you say so.

What if Jesus tells us to try something different? What if he asks us to try one more time? Will we say we're too tired, we've already tried, or we just want to go home to Christian families and friends?

Or will we let down our nets once more, this time trying it his way?

Those fishermen gathered their now-clean nets, their tired bodies, and their weary minds. They boarded their boats and set out for deep water. And they let down their nets once more. This is when it got irrational, for as they followed Jesus' instructions, they caught so many fish their nets began to break, and they called over other boats to help them haul in their catch.

We can and will be effective at our call to be fishers of men and women only so far as we trust in Jesus and implement his new, old ways.

Updating the Methods

At Alpha, we have the benefit of working with around 6,500 churches in the United States and more than 30,000 churches globally. In the US alone, an estimated 426,000 people went through Alpha courses in 2019, globally, almost 1.5 million. We're connected to every major Christian denomination, from Catholic to Protestant, charismatic to Baptist, Calvinist to Armenian, contemporary to traditional, and everything and everyone in-between. We are seeing some of what is working and some of what isn't—we've been casting a lot of nets. I can confidently say from our broad viewpoint, these shifts we're about to discuss will effectively turn the trends of evangelism around. With these shifts, you will mobilize Millennials and younger Christians to share their faith and help us all reach people who feel far from God.

In the coming pages, you'll be introduced to churches, pastors, and lay people who have revived evangelism in each of their contexts by implementing a few of these shifts. I'll unpack how these timely approaches are rooted in the timelessness of Jesus: his ways, not just my ideas. Additionally, in each of the chapters, we'll build these shifts from the wisdom gleaned in the Barna/Alpha USA "Reviving Evangelism" study (an exhaustive research project that compared evangelism experiences and expectations of Christians and non-Christians—sort of like a report on the current state of evangelism in the US). Combining this data, our macro viewpoint in Alpha, and the timeless insight of Christ, I think, will illuminate a better way forward.

At the end of each chapter I've included a section called, "What's Next?" Here, we'll explore various questions having to do with each chapter topic—you can go through each of these on your own, but I recommend you process your answers with someone else. My goal for the "What's Next?" section is for all of us to unpack our deeply held views on evangelism and find the freedom to change what we're doing, eliminate harmful practices, and, at the end of the day, lead our loved ones and fellow community members to Christ.

You can do it, too, you know. You can change the way you approach evangelism. You don't have to dismantle everything you're currently doing at your church or in your life, but by rethinking some of your strategies, you can see a renewal of people outside the church coming to a new life through Jesus Christ.

Can we trust Jesus enough to follow him in old, new ways? That is the call, even in the midst of this difficult place the Western church finds itself. That is the answer that can turn the tide.

Trust in Jesus and his ways to reach those whom he loves and longs for.

What Next?

- What is your past experience in evangelism? What is your current experience of evangelism?
- How tightly are you holding on to traditional evangelistic methods? Are you willing to loosen your grip on them and try something new?
- List the evangelism ministries and events you've tried. Are there other methods you think the Lord might be asking you to try, but you've put them off out of fear?
- Spend some time in prayer asking the Lord for wisdom when it comes to evangelism, a willingness to try things the Jesus way, and an open mind and heart as you read further in this book.

Hungry for More, Not Just Hoping for Many

I had a stark realization a few years back, and it came out of the blue: My son's faith was on autopilot. He was around 10 years old at the time, intellectual for his age, curious, fun, and generally shy but good at making close friends. He would often process things on his own and then come back with a well-developed, independent view that he felt strongly about. He has always been very sensitive to those around him.

He grew up in the church, knew his Bible inside out, and had absorbed more information about Christianity than just about anyone else his age. It's possible he knew more than many adult Christians. I had intentionally tried to make sure the beauty of the Christian faith was accessible to him from the time he was born. We prayed together; we read the Bible together; we had spiritual conversations often. As a Christian father, one of the things I care most about is introducing my own children to Jesus in a way that will lead them into a lifelong relationship with him.

And yet.

There was simply no real evidence that my son had grown to deeply embrace any of it. I'm not saying he was turning into a rebel. But the Christian spirituality that developed as he grew up was primarily a head-level, cultural kind of faith. He knew the words to the worship songs, but I wasn't sure they had penetrated his heart. He knew what to say and when to say it, but I wasn't always so sure he actually believed it. He knew the answers to most of the questions, but I wondered if he was simply saying what I wanted him to say.

Something seemed to be missing, and I wondered if he had a heart-level relationship with his Creator.

Have you ever desired Christ for someone else so intensely it hurt? Have you ever wept for someone, wishing so badly they would have a life-changing encounter with Jesus, the kind you experienced once upon a time? Have you ever prayed long into the night for someone you loved, or for your congregation, or for your community, with a desire so strong you were unable to sleep? That's what I carried during those days.

My son didn't seem to enjoy church that much, or many things connected to faith, but he happened to be born into a family where faith mattered, so he continued to show up and do what was expected of him. He went through the motions. He rarely complained. But I could tell that he didn't have much genuine interest when it came to connecting with God.

When I realized this about my son, I started praying for him more intently, more deliberately, more consistently than I had ever prayed for anything before. I would close my eyes at night and see his face, remember what he had been like as a toddler and a preschooler, and I hoped his heart would turn toward the Lord. I prayed over and over again that the content that had seeped into him through the years would materialize and become meaningful.

Maybe you can relate to the place where my son was. I know I can. There are stretches of our spiritual journeys, sometimes long stretches, where our faith takes a back seat to the day-to-day concerns of living. Or when church doesn't feel worth it. Or when God feels absent and irrelevant to what's going on in the world.

This realization about my son came over a period of time, but it all seemed to culminate for me on a prayer and worship night at our church. We were having a series of meetings designed for people to take some time and draw closer to God, and during one of those services, my desire for my son to experience God overwhelmed me. It was a deeper longing than I had ever known before, that his heart would be captured by Jesus. It was a visceral sensation; one I could feel deep in my gut.

On that night, I entered into this space of deep travail and earnest prayer at a level I'd not known. I pleaded. I prayed. I worshiped. I begged. Again and again and again. In the midst of this deep and meaningful moment, the

Holy Spirit's voice emerged. I got the message loud and clear, but it was a message I hadn't expected.

What you see in him is what I see in you.

Wait, I thought. *What are you saying, God?*

What you see in him is what I see in you. You see a surface-level faith in your son, but why would he have anything else, when that's what you have—a surface-level faith.

It was so clear to me what the Holy Spirit was saying, and it cut right to my heart.

This going through the motions, this head-level discipleship, this mediocre hunger for the Lord isn't just his problem. It's your too. The lack of intimacy with God, the shallow experiences of his presence, the quick prayers, the run-of-the-mill desires . . . this isn't just in the life of this person you care about.

It's all through your life too.

I physically collapsed to the floor. I was broken open in prayer for the sake of my own soul, not for my salvation but simply because I had lost my first love. I realized in that moment I had become lukewarm.

"You say, 'I am rich; I have acquired wealth and do not need a thing.' But you do not realize that you are wretched, pitiful, poor, blind and naked" (Revelation 3:17).

That was me. I was the one who needed a clearer sense of God's presence, a greater desire for him.

If I wanted my son to come alive in Christ, I couldn't simply hope for that to happen for him—I needed to hunger for more, for me.

This changed the trajectory of my life.

I dug deep for many months, entered into a much more profound prayer life, longed for the Lord, asked for more, and, as much as I could, put aside the shallow monotony of faith.

My cry for revival in someone else had to shift into a cry for revival within me.

The Problem with Hoping for Many

As Christians, most of us can connect with the hope that many will come to know Jesus. We look around at the world, at all the things that seem to be going wrong, and we want Jesus to enter into those situations and change everything for the good. We cross paths with hurting people and, because we have experienced the transformation that Christ can bring, we want them to experience it too. We spend time with people we love and wish they could experience God in new and amazing ways.

Please, God, we pray, *make a difference in the lives of the people around me, draw them to yourself, Jesus!*

The next natural step is to start asking ourselves how we can make this happen. *What are the things we can do? What should we say? What books can we give them? What inspiring videos do they need to see? What meme or truth-telling photo can I share on Facebook or Instagram which will transform them this instant?*

Maybe not that last one. But anyway, we're convinced there has to be some logical path we can follow in order to introduce our friends and loved ones to Christ or to help

25

those who know him in a shallow way to go deeper. We start to believe that in order to make that happen, in order to be effective evangelists to those who feel lost, in order to have churches that bring many people to Christ, we should focus all our effort on outward-facing activities.

What programs can we create that will interest many?

How can we talk to our friends in order to turn their hearts toward God?

How can we fill up our churches?

Where and when should we host some kind of outreach effort to reach our community?

And of course, I have to say: This isn't a wrong desire. We *should* hope that many come to know Christ. We *should* be in prayer for our family and friends. We *should* have heavy hearts for the lost in our communities and long to see our world transformed. We *should* do something about it. This is a natural desire for Christians, especially in those of us who have been transformed by Christ. After all, it's called good news—naturally, we want more people to hear it.

But often our hope for many can drift into a lesser motivation than what the Lord wants for us. It can even morph into a broken motivation, especially when it's tied to attendance numbers or offering totals or personal evangelism guilt appeasement or notches on our eternal evangelism belts.

What lies at the heart of our hope for many?

Is it that the seats in our half-full auditoriums would be filled?

Is it that the dwindling offerings would be revived?

Is it so that I can stop feeling ashamed for a while about the unfulfilled command, "Go, and make disciples . . ."?

Hoping for many isn't a wrong desire, but it is the wrong starting point.

What God wants even more than for us to hope for many is for us to hunger for him.

Ultimately, the ignited love of the Lord within us is what draws other people to him. We can't let our primary motivation be *only* the urgency of the gospel or the command to go and share so that many will hear and be saved.

Our evangelism efforts must be more deeply rooted than that.

We have to hunger for God for ourselves more than we ever have before.

Our desire for revival must begin with the cry, "Revive me!"

In the heart of New York City sits a church called Church of the City, pastored by Jon Tyson. Jon is a deep well of genuine lived faith and urban leadership. He has a powerful hunger for prayer. These things are placing Church of the City on the front lines of evangelism in one of the most post-Christian cities in America.

One of the temptations for those of us who, like Jon, live in heavily post-Christian contexts might be to believe the desire for spirituality just isn't there, that the world around us has lost its desire for spiritual things. That's simply not the case. Even in the settings which seem to be the most post-Christian, people have thriving spiritual thirst. Did you know that 47 percent of urban non-Christians and lapsed Christians have unanswered spiritual questions? Or that 39 percent of that same group say they are "seeking something spiritually better"? And nearly 4 out of 10 are "on a quest for spiritual truth."[1] As I mentioned earlier, Millennial non-Christians report being twice as likely than older non-Christians to learn more about the Christian faith and its impact on their lives.[2]

What does this data tell us?

A large group of people who no longer go to church are still open, even longing, for the gospel in the heart of a deeply post-Christian environment.

Enter Jon Tyson, who launched Church of the City with this idea in mind: He wanted to ignite a passion for people to contend for spiritual awakening in our time. What an incredible crossroads between a strong desire for the transformation of the world and for a church movement!

Jon doesn't dream small. Jon's family doesn't dream small, either. Most families take vacations to Disney World or spend their leisure time at the beach. Recently, Jon and his family went on a trip, but it wasn't to Epcot—they embarked on a journey to visit some of the most prominent locations of Christian revival over the last few centuries.[3]

But what does the word *revival* even mean? What does it look like?

To answer those questions, Jon points us to an insight from Jonathan Edwards: "Revival is the acceleration and intensification of the normal work of the Holy Spirit so that as much is done in a day or two, as at ordinary times . . . is done in a year."[4]

That sounds good, right? We want things to happen faster, we want our entire city to fall in love with Jesus . . . today. We want our loved ones to follow Jesus . . . yesterday. But there is a process that leads to revival, or so concludes Jon studying the history and paths of so many well-known revivals.

First comes *regeneration*. This usually arrives in the form of conviction, in which we see our need for God, Jesus, and the cross. We're given the righteousness of God and become new creatures in Christ. It's the kind of personal revival that introduces us to a life in Christ and begins the process of opening our eyes to the truth. It's the movement that begins with the cry, *"Lord, revive me!"*

Second comes a process of *restoration*, during which God, in his unfailing kindness, begins to bring back the things that were lost when we lived apart from him. Maybe it's finances or family, relationships or health. Perhaps you have experienced this, and you realize what a beautiful thing it is, this restoration power.

Third comes *reformation*. This is a time of struggle and engagement with God unlike anything you've experienced before. You will probably become aware of your old ways of living and have a strong desire to walk in the Spirit. During this stage, we put on Christ and put away the flesh, but only by the grace and power of God. This becomes a time of incredible spiritual maturity.

From there we move into *renewal*, where we experience a dynamic energy that isn't the result of human leadership but of the supernatural, legitimate working of the Spirit.

This can be a tremendously exciting time where fresh energy comes and fills us and the churches we inhabit. Maybe you've witnessed times of renewal, perhaps in prayer or church planting or some other phase, during which you could sense a palpable excitement gathering around the work of God.

After regeneration, restoration, reformation, and renewal comes *revival*. During revival, the number of people who normally come to Christ in a twenty-year period come to Christ in two months. Everything is accelerated. In fact, so much happens in such a short time, and so many people decide to explore and follow Christ, that our normal ways of doing things cannot contain the work that's taking place. Churches overflow. Lives change. Cue the imagery of those early disciples trying to haul in the nets.

After all of these, *awakening* is possible. This is when God transforms an entire culture.[5]

The moral of the story is that you can't leap directly into revival or awakening. We all want to see this kind of incredible awakening sweep through our families, our cities, our nations, and our cultures. We all want to see churches filled and hearts in untold numbers turn to Jesus.

But we must first travel the path, and it begins with regeneration, or personal renewal.

But Jesus Often Withdrew

How do we get to that place—where can we go to find this transformational renewal for our own souls so that we, in turn, can see those around us find Christ?

There is something Jesus did consistently throughout his ministry, something that served as a foundation for the way he lived, and it is one of the main experiences we can use to spark the flames of revival in our own lives. The gospel writers don't waste any time introducing us to it: We see this practice of Jesus twice in the first chapter of Mark, first in verses 12 and 13:

> At once the Spirit sent him out into the wilderness, and he was in the wilderness forty days, being tempted by Satan. He was with the wild animals, and angels attended him.

And then again in verses 35–37:

> Very early in the morning, while it was still dark, Jesus got up, left the house and went off to a solitary place, where he prayed. Simon and his companions went to look for him, and when they found him, they exclaimed: "Everyone is looking for you!"

It's so interesting to me, during the early days of Jesus' ministry, that he clearly made a habit of going off on his own to seek God through prayer, fasting, and solitude. Jesus knew there was value in spending time alone with God . . . and he was fully God! Even being part of the Trinity, Jesus still needed that communal time with God the Father. How much more do we need to break away from the daily grind, pull ourselves away from the grip of our mobile phones and laptops and televisions, and spend one-on-one time with our Creator?

As the gospels continue, we start to see how often these times of personal spirituality are followed by major miracles. Consider Mark 6:45–50:

> Immediately Jesus made his disciples get into the boat and go on ahead of him to Bethsaida, while he dismissed the crowd. After leaving them, he went up on a mountainside to pray. Later that night, the boat was in the middle of the lake, and he was alone on land. He saw the disciples straining at the oars, because the wind was against them. Shortly before dawn he went out to them, walking on the lake. He was about to pass by them, but when they saw him walking on the lake, they thought he was a ghost. They cried out, because they all saw him and were terrified. Immediately he spoke to them and said, "Take courage! It is I. Don't be afraid."

Did you catch it there? In one lonely little verse, pinned between two major miracles (with Jesus feeding the 5,000 and Jesus walking on water), it says that "he went up on a mountainside to pray." Jesus was doing these incredible things, miracles no one had seen before, and even in the midst of the miraculous, he maintained a foundation of prayer and intimacy with his heavenly Father.

Hold on to that for a second, and check out another passage, Luke 5:12–16:

While Jesus was in one of the towns, a man came along who was covered with leprosy. When he saw Jesus, he fell with his face to the ground and begged him, "Lord, if you are willing, you can make me clean." Jesus reached out his hand and touched the man. "I am willing," he said. "Be clean!" And immediately the leprosy left him. Then Jesus ordered him, "Don't tell anyone, but go, show yourself to the priest and offer the sacrifices that Moses commanded for your cleansing, as a testimony to them." Yet the news about him spread all the more, so that crowds of people came to hear him and to be healed of their sicknesses. But Jesus often withdrew to lonely places and prayed.

Did you catch it there again? "But Jesus often withdrew to lonely places and prayed." Flocks of people were trying to track down Jesus. Crowds wanted to find out more about him. Potential followers were desperate to see him. Yet in the midst of what many of us would see as a great gospel opportunity to lead more people to the truth, Jesus didn't let this fame or even this potential to do good take precedence over his prayer life.

And one final example, from Matthew 26:36–39:

Then Jesus went with his disciples to a place called Gethsemane, and he said to them, "Sit here while I go over there and pray." He took Peter and the two sons of Zebedee along with him, and he began to be sorrowful and troubled. Then he said to them,

33

"My soul is overwhelmed with sorrow to the point of death. Stay here and keep watch with me." Going a little farther, he fell with his face to the ground and prayed, "My Father, if it is possible, may this cup be taken from me. Yet not as I will, but as you will."

There, in one of the most desperate moments of Jesus' life, during the hours leading up to his torture and brutal crucifixion, he went out alone, falling onto his face, praying. Jesus could have done many things in order to prepare himself and the budding movement of the future church for the difficult path ahead, but he chose to go and pray.

This is not an exhaustive list of the times Jesus went out on his own to pray. He was literally doing it all the time. He knew that if he was going to be able to sustain the incredible revival that was taking place during his time, he needed periods of personal renewal, solitude, and intimate connection with the Father. He experienced a revival within himself, and the revival became evident and expanded to all around him.

This isn't just about having a quick quiet time and worship gathering before you go out to evangelize. I'm not talking about some kind of check-the-box habit which helps us feel as though we are doing our duty. This withdrawal, this inner work, must come out of a specific motivation: becoming intimate with the Father.

Didn't Jesus want many to know the Father? Didn't he talk wistfully of wanting to gather all people close to himself? Of course he did! He was active. He was preaching and teaching all the time. He was instructing his disciples constantly. He was on the go. He was healing people and casting out demons and mingling with the crowds. I'm not arguing that we should all become desert monks and retreat into the wilderness indefinitely or only attend prayer and worship gatherings while waiting for people to come to us.

But when Jesus engaged with people, the interaction rose up out of his insatiable passion and hunger for intimacy with the Father.

I know withdrawing can feel like a risk, especially in this day and age of connectedness, celebrity pastor status, and social media. To disappear from the world around us even for a day, to take time away from activist efforts for soul-filling worship and prayer, can feel like a massive roll of the dice. It might even seem irresponsible.

So many people are depending on us!

Who will keep things going?

Who will build friendships, reach the lost, and serve the city?

It's easy to be afraid that by pulling back, we'll let people down.

Will our unsaved friends forget about us if we try to spend time focusing on our own relationship with God?

Will churches disintegrate if the lead pastors pour themselves out in lengthy times of prayer?

Will the crowds that have gathered in our churches evaporate when we put our catchy sermon series aside in order to make sure we're cultivating unstoppable passion for Jesus within the church?

In some counterintuitive sense, we have to release the hope for many to know him or show up in our churches, and instead take the required time to ensure the richness of hunger in our own hearts. Worship, prayer, fasting, and more prayer and more after that—whatever it takes to achieve that level of hunger for him within ourselves.

Nothing of lasting impact will come apart from us seeking deeper intimacy with Jesus.

Where Do We Find Revival?

The problem with words like *revival* and *awakening* is that it can all seem so huge, so incomprehensible. Even if we bring it down to the personal level, focusing on seeking revival for ourselves, it's easy to be left feeling overwhelmed and not knowing where to begin.

Here are steps Tyson suggests might help you begin to drill down into a desire for personal revival:[6]

1. *Prepare for, and embrace, the crystallization of discontent.* The phrase "crystallization of discontent" is used by psychologists to describe the moment when someone decides they are unhappy enough about something to make a change. It's the moment when a battered woman declares she doesn't care how nice her abuser might sometimes be, she's leaving. It's when someone wakes up one day and realizes beyond a shadow of a doubt that they're in a cult and they have to get out. It's that point in time when a man looks in the mirror and admits he is an alcoholic and has to get help.

You can see this happen in the book of Nehemiah, where the people have been languishing for decades, numb in their ruin. Only when Nehemiah arrives and asks about the exiles do they wake from that haze and decide to make a change.

Prepare your heart for this. Ask God to bring you crystallization of discontent, where you can no longer bear staying the same and you begin to desire him more than anything else in your life.

2. *Be willing to see your personal inadequacy.* One of the great things that God can do for you is to help you see your personal inadequacy. Of course, this can be a painful experience at first, because all of us spend most of our lives trying very hard to remain blind to our inadequacy! We are, for all intents and purposes, able to remain happier on a surface level when we think we have more or less already "arrived."

This is what happened to me when I started seeking God for my son. I had my eyes on my son's inadequacy, my son's weakness, my son's need for renewal in Jesus, but when I pressed into God, the first thing God did was to turn my eyes to my own weakness. At that point, it would have been easy for me to deny that, to keep trying to refocus on the changes I wanted to see in my son's life. But when I allowed God to point out what was lacking in me, the embers of a personal revival were lit.

3. *Seek God in new ways.* If you're not feeling the discontent crystallizing, if you're unable to see your own personal inadequacy, try seeking God in new ways. Practice spiritual

disciplines you have never practiced before—prayer, fasting, Bible study, meditation, service, worship. Read books by authors you haven't read. Dig into specific books of the Bible that in the past you've found boring or difficult. Attend passionate prayer gatherings you never would have said yes to and at times you never would have agreed to.

Seeking God in new ways can open up your mind to new revelations, or perhaps old revelations in new forms. This can be an effective way to spark revival in yourself.

4. *Rededicate yourself to a life of prayer.* One of the most potent ways to stir up a new experience with God and to spur on revival is to dedicate yourself to a life of prayer. When Jon Tyson and his team at Church of the City realized this, they began to reorganize the life of their church around prayer. Now, they have four different hours of corporate prayer available every day. They allocate about a quarter of a million dollars a year to prayer programs and the staff required to support them. On New Year's Eve, they have an all-night prayer service. People have come into their church saying they couldn't pray for five minutes, attend an all-night prayer service, and realize they can pray all night long.

They've decided prayer is going to be the heart and foundation of everything they do. What would it look like for you to reorient your life or your church around prayer? How would that change the way you lived? How would that stir a hunger for more in you?

5. *Reorient your life around this desire for personal revival.* The truth is that unless you make some changes in your life and dig into this new desire for God, you're probably not

going to experience the kind of inner renewal and revival you need to see those around you come to Jesus. Rachel and Abby both moved to New York City with successful, fast-paced careers in marketing. They were both unexpectedly seized with a divine heartbreak for the state of the Western church, so they attended an all-night prayer meeting. That's when they realized they could be great women of intercession, so they moved in order to be within a two-minute walk of the prayer room. They led a small group at Church of the City that grew from 15 people to 160 people, many of whom not only grew their hunger for more of God but also said yes to following Jesus. And these were two "ordinary" young women in their mid-twenties who happened to live in a city we might stereotype as difficult to reach for Jesus. The only difference in them was that they decided to reorient their lives around their desire for revival.

If you have a desire for those around you to discover Jesus, if you are heartbroken for the state of the church and want to see our culture fall in love with Christ, and if you can recognize that this revival must first begin in you, make some of these changes in your life.

Any meaningful revival must begin within us.

My Personal Revival

So, what happened with my son and me?

Well, I took the word of the Holy Spirit seriously—I started to seek God through various spiritual disciplines.

I stopped focusing on my son's relationship with God (although I never stopped incessantly praying for him) and became more concerned with my own journey with Jesus. I began seeking revival inside of me.

And I experienced a spiritual renewal unlike anything I had experienced before in my life.

Soon after that, I began to see movement in the faith of my son. It started small. It wasn't anything remarkable, not at first, but we actually started praying together regularly. We traveled as a family to the home of the Alpha program in England, and during that trip, I had the opportunity to witness a deepening of his faith.

While our spiritual journey spread itself out over time, it all culminated at a healing service our family attended (which was something new for us). My wife had experienced back pain for nine years, something that no doctor or specialist could treat effectively, and while we were at this healing service, my son decided to pray for her.

It was one of the most powerful experiences of my life, seeing my son, growing into a young man, praying for his mother. And her back pain stopped (and still hasn't returned). I don't know what you believe about that sort of thing, but I'm reminded of the blind man in John 9:25, "One thing I do know. I was blind but now I see!"

This created a new openness to prayer in all of us, a stronger hunger for God, and when we returned from the trip, my son decided on his own that he wanted to be baptized.

He had a beautiful baptism celebration, and that's

when I started to see what happens when we experience personal renewal: My son invited a friend to a church gathering, and this non-Christian friend of his came along. Soon after that, my son began inviting more friends to church, and some of them are now growing toward Christ. My son is praying and reading Scripture regularly with me and has had an alive relationship with Jesus since that time.

We might want to see many come to Christ, and that is a beautiful desire to have, but the origin is always a renewal of our own hearts.

Maybe you picked up this book out of a desire to lead many to Jesus—that's not a wrong desire. I'm so glad you're coming on this journey with me!

But, again, that good desire is actually the wrong starting point.

All the great revivalists in history first discovered their own personal renewal.

Seek God with everything in you—renew your intimacy with him at a greater level, for no reason other than to know his face. He is the great reward.

This is the first step.

Before we begin this journey into evangelism, let's make sure we get our hearts in the right place; we must hunger for more before we hope for many. As our own hearts are ignited, then we can effectively draw others into the warming love of Christ and take this next step in effectively sharing Christ.

What Next?

- List a handful of specific people you would love to see make the decision to follow Jesus.
- Which of the steps in personal revival series listed above seem most compelling to you?
- What are a few practical things you could do in order to seek God in new ways and jumpstart your own personal revival?

Conversation, Not Just Proclamation

T here's a woman, and she's never stepped foot inside a church before, mostly because she always found them intimidating and mysterious and somewhat irrelevant. When she was a little girl in her parents' car driving past church buildings, they always felt otherworldly to her— maybe it was their neighboring graveyards, or the midweek empty parking lots, or the gaping windows, or the cross situated up on the steeple, or the strange ways Christians in town treated her and her family. Whatever the case, she decided at some point in her life that she would just as soon stay away than walk through those doors.[1]

Years passed, and a friend invited her to an Alpha course held at the friend's church. They said it was a series of gatherings for people like her to ask questions and share perspectives about spiritual things: a time to hang out and eat a meal and meet other people who wanted to have meaningful conversations.

Admittedly, it took her a minute to get comfortable with the idea—churches still freaked her out. But she was older by then, and the invite itself was enough to lower her defenses. She said yes, she would go along. She was nervous in the days leading up to it, and all of her childhood fears and anxieties about church almost kept her from going. But not quite. When she showed up, it wasn't even to the first meeting in the Alpha series—the course was already nearing the end of its run. But this church, this space that she expected to be scary and religious and filled with people who thought they knew it all, surprised her.

That place turned out to be full of human beings who loved to laugh, liked to have a good time, and enjoyed earnest conversations about life and faith. At first, she sat in silence, but she was completely disarmed by their kindness, their welcome, their lack of judgment and correction of others, and the unconditional friendship they offered. She found herself opening up, telling her own story, and listening to the stories of others as they meandered along this path.

She gave her life to Jesus by the end of the course. After that, she started attending church.

"I never knew church could be like this," she told her new pastor, smiling. "There are normal people here! And it's a place that values truth-seeking. It doesn't feel hostile at all."

Her pastor is my friend, Drew Hyun, and he plants churches in New York City. Alpha has become a big part of their evangelism strategy.

In his words, "There's a high level of skepticism in New York City for anything big or slick or produced. People have a lot of questions, a lot of doubt, whenever anyone else is trying to share something from a stage or a platform. People here are looking for a far more authentic texture when it comes to truth and relationship."

While it may fall at an extreme end of the spectrum, New York City doesn't sound that much different from the rest of the country or many other cities scattered around the world, does it? As more and more people become skeptical of the church, and as Millennials and Gen Z become less comfortable sharing the gospel, we've entered an age where resistance to any sort of proclamation is reaching an all-time high.

"Most of the people I know who have converted to Christianity," Drew went on to explain to me, "didn't do it because of the form. They didn't do it because of this container of the Sunday morning experience. It wasn't because of how good the preacher was or how impressive the worship was."

So why do people come to faith? What is it that draws them in?

"Well, in my experience," Drew continued, "they eventually became a Christian because someone said to them, 'Hey, do you want to have dinner together? Let's talk about matters of faith and life. I'd love to hear your thoughts.'"

In other words, they weren't drawn to Christianity by proclamation alone.

They found their way into faith through conversation.

The Problem with Proclamation Alone

There's something very peculiar about the way Jesus chose to interact with people during his short time on earth: The Bible records 307 questions that Jesus asked, along with 183 questions others asked of him—but do you know how many times Jesus gave a direct answer?[2]

Eight.

Eight times.

And some scholars argue that on only three of those occasions was the answer he gave completely direct.

Jesus was 40 times more likely to ask a question than to provide a direct answer (give or take). And this, coming from the one and only person who walked the earth and actually knew all the answers.

Maybe you're wondering, *So what?* Maybe you're wondering what Jesus' tendency to deflect questions or craft a longer conversation has to do with evangelism today. Maybe you're wondering how we even got here.

Questions and answers.

What does this have to do with the Great Commission?

This: Jesus' propensity to ask questions, or to leave the questions of others unanswered, is a profoundly different type of evangelism than that on which most churches around the globe have been built in the last 50 years. I think it's fair to say that as a worldwide church, we have somehow depended almost entirely on proclamation as the definitive evangelism strategy. For a time, it seemed to work. There were, after all, stadiums and large gatherings of people who, under the proclamations of well-known evangelists, found Jesus (and this is still effective in some parts of the world). There have been those reached through proclamation on the radio and television and in churches and, more recently, on the internet.

We are, most of us, answerers and answer-seekers. We want to know the right answer so that we can say the right things. We are, most of us, trained to respond to gaps in anyone's theology with the hammer of truth, nailing our knowledge home.

I know this is true because I was a pastor for many years. We relied almost entirely on proclamation alone. Ours was a large church, and we invested millions of dollars every single year on one main proclamation event.

Maybe you've heard of it?

It's known as the Sunday morning service.

Our goal was to attract into our services people who were exploring faith, and once we had them there, we proclaimed the truth through worship songs and sermons. If the Sunday morning service didn't entice them, we created compelling outreach events and proclaimed the truth to them there. We also trained up personal evangelists within the congregation and sent them to their friends and families and coworkers, all with one goal: Proclaim the good news.

Proclamation, proclamation, proclamation.

Before you hastily close the book and call me a heretic, thinking that I'm promoting a model of evangelism based on wordless example, let me say this: proclamation is a necessary part of the strategy for spreading the gospel and it always will be. Romans 10:14 remains just as true today as ever before:

> "How, then, can they call on the one they have not believed in? And how can they believe in the one of whom they have not heard?"

Proclamation is important. Speaking truth is imperative. Using our words to introduce people to Jesus is still crucial. Many have the good news proclaimed to them in one form or another, and many of those respond with a heart-resounding, "Yes!"—just as I did during a proclamation event in a church some 25 years ago.

But not everyone.

First, there are hundreds of thousands of people in a close radius of your church and mine who are flat-out unwilling to show up to our proclamation gatherings, ever. Then, there are hundreds of thousands of people who are unwilling to engage in personal conversations where they are just being preached at. And, as the years have passed, our proclamations have become even less relevant to the world around us. Many of our faith proclamations are no longer addressing the questions of the culture.

We're proclaiming truths that answer the questions:

How can I be forgiven for my sin?

How can I know I'll go to heaven?

How can you prove God exists?

But, by and large, those aren't the questions being asked anymore. Nowadays, the questions sound more like:

How can I find purpose?

How can I deal with loneliness and emptiness?

What will help me live a great life now, not in some distant afterlife, but here and now?

Where can I find an answer to the injustices in this broken world?

Recently, at an Alpha gathering, a young man, a self-prescribed atheist, turned to me and said something that caught my attention: "If I believed God was real and I could ask one question, I'd ask God what I could do with my life that significantly matters."

The questions are shifting.

Also, today's discourse is inflamed. As I mentioned earlier, our findings in the *Reviving Evangelism* study indicated a 100 percent jump from GenXers to Millennials in adherence to this statement: *Disagreement is interpreted as judgment.* A new tribalism in every sector of our society has emerged. Us versus Them.

You don't need data to convince you of this. Just look on social media and you'll see the polarization play out in real time over virtually any topic. You have each side of the political spectrum lobbing verbal grenades at one another while entrenching deeper into their own echo chambers. We have the vaccinate or never vaccinate tribes. The climate change and the no climate change debate. The Chevy versus Ford debacle. The vegans and meat eaters are even going at it—I like to call it the beets versus smoked meats. I'm in the smoked meats camp, in case you were wondering (my wife, Sarah, is a vegetarian which always makes mealtime interesting).

Certainly, this culture of vehement disagreement has spilled over into the religion and faith conversations of the day. We've lost the art of discourse in our time, and proclamation alone only perpetuates this contemporary problem. If someone has a legitimate question in a disagreement-equals-judgment culture when it comes to faith, and we respond with a quick one-sided, one-dimensional, one-directional proclamation of hard truth, we won't get from question number one, which is lodged in the head of the asker, to questions five and six, which are lodged in the heart.

With proclamation as our primary model, the dialogue ends far too soon, and people retreat to their respective corners, all congratulating themselves on a rhetorical victory, all wondering why their "win" feels so hollow.

Jesus and a Different Approach

So, if people aren't as open to straight-up proclamation, what are they looking for? How are they attempting to find answers to the big questions of life? What or who are they turning to when life is difficult, or they are staring down their own mortality without any sense of significance?

This resistance to proclamation isn't only found on our city streets or back country roads. Proclamation alone hasn't only lost some of its power in the secular world. It's also becoming less and less effective within our churches, as greater connectivity online introduces all of us to more and more questions, more and more immersion into our post-Christian culture and worldview, and more and more cause for doubt. There's a huge desire building in those sitting in our church pews or logging on to our digital sermons to ask questions, to engage in conversations about faith, the Bible, and Christianity.

But if we continue the proclamation-only model, where will people go in our churches when they have serious questions to ask?

Will people wrestling with questions find space and welcome, or will they be met with more simplistic answers and a sense of spoken or unspoken judgment in response to their doubt? Is there a space in our evangelism strategies for conversation, or are we only providing platforms of proclamation? People in our culture, and even those in our churches, increasingly seek out places of conversation. We can, and we must, go back to Jesus' style of evangelism, but it's going to require us to re-prioritize one of the most vital, yet overlooked, skills that Jesus possessed.

The skill of listening.

What if Christians were 40 times more likely to respond to questions and doubts and disagreements with listening (just like Jesus)? What if Christians asked 40 questions and thoughtfully listened to the responses for every one proclamation (just like Jesus)? What if Christians were the best listeners on the planet, reshaping and retraining culture to become effective listeners of one another (just like Jesus)? If so, we would begin to reflect the heart and behavior of Jesus with more clarity and draw more people into a relationship with Jesus with more consistency.

The Power of Listening

There's a fascinating passage in the gospel of John (1:29–34) that shows the power of listening (while at the same time reminding us of the importance of proclamation). It all starts when John the Baptist sees Jesus.

> The next day John saw Jesus coming toward him and said, "Look, the Lamb of God, who takes away the sin of the world! This is the one I meant when I said, 'A man who comes after me has surpassed me because he was before me.' I myself did not know him, but the reason I came baptizing with water was that he might be revealed to Israel."
>
> Then John gave this testimony: "I saw the Spirit come down from heaven as a dove and remain on him. And I myself did not know him, but the one who sent me to baptize with water told me, 'The man on whom you see the Spirit come down and remain is the one who will baptize with the Holy Spirit.' I have seen and I testify that this is God's Chosen One."

John is proclaiming that Jesus is the Lamb of God, God's Chosen One.

But what happens next is interesting.

The following day, John says the same thing, "Look, the Lamb of God!" And two of John's disciples hear him say this. They're curious. They start walking after Jesus. As Jewish people in that era, they would probably have known how loaded that phrase was—"The Lamb of God"—and they wanted to know more.

As they follow Jesus, he stops and turns around. He looks at them. And he says his first recorded words in the gospel of John.

They arrive, interestingly enough, in the form of a question.

"What do you want?"

A few other translations interpret the question as, "What do you seek?" or, "What are you looking for?"

What jumps out to me is that, when confronted with his status as the Lamb of God—a phrase packed with all kinds of lighting-rod religious and political implications—Jesus didn't choose to go into an exegesis of Old Testament prophecy or lay out the many ways he was fulfilling it. Jesus didn't delve into a three-point sermon on the symbolism of the Lamb of God or what that would mean for him and his followers. Jesus didn't talk about how they needed to change their lives, begin formulating a list of rules, or lay out the many characteristics they would need to give up if they were to follow him.

He asked a simple question, engaging in a conversation with them. He was drawing out their hearts, trying to get to the bottom of their thoughts, desires, and lives. And in doing so, Jesus provides the space for them to respond with a question of their own in verse 38. Their response is almost as telling as his question.

"Rabbi," they asked, "where are you staying?"

Jesus, how can we find you?

Jesus, where can we go to be with you?

Jesus, we want to know more.

What they wanted was not for Jesus to proclaim who he was or what John meant when he called him the Lamb of God.

What they wanted was to find out where he was staying—to be with him.

What if Jesus shut down their process with a hard-and-fast proclamation in that moment when what they simply wanted was to spend time with him—to begin journeying with him?

And when Jesus replied, "Come and see," he was telling them that he didn't want to just transfer intellectual property to them or answer their questions with analysis. Jesus wasn't interested in having them immediately consent to certain truths about him or who he was.

Jesus wanted to walk together with them in relationship.

"What do you want?"

"Where are you staying?"

"Come and see."

Jesus knew that a powerhouse proclamation right there by the Jordan River would most likely not lead them into an all-out life transformation. He knew that kind of change would require walking together—a series of conversations, rooted in listening, and spanning over time.

The ultimate invitation is to walk with him. To experience him.

The very first words of Jesus in the gospel of John do not come to us in the form of a proclamation—they arrive as a question that tries to get at the heart of who we are, followed by an invitation into an ongoing conversation and relationship journey with him.

One of the most fascinating stats from the *Reviving Evangelism* study had to do with the top qualities spiritually curious non-Christians in America are looking for in a person with whom to talk about faith.[3]

First and foremost was someone who "listens without judgment." Spiritually curious people want to be able to bring things up, introduce controversial topics and doubts, and ask questions without feeling like Christians are judging every word they're saying or dismissing them because of a long-held belief. In fact, 62 percent of non-Christians and lapsed Christians say that someone who listens without judgment would be the best person to talk with about faith: significantly higher than any other quality reported.

The second most desired quality?

"Does not force me to draw a conclusion." Half of all non-Christians and lapsed Christians think this is a trait of someone who would be a helpful person to talk to about faith.

If you read the gospels through this lens, you'll see that this is the Jesus way. He is constantly drawing people into conversations, listening, abstaining from judgment, and allowing the person to come to conclusions on their own.

Unfortunately, only 34 percent of lapsed and non-Christians say some of the Christians they know listen without judgment. And only 26 percent say some of the Christians they know allow them to come to their own conclusions.[4] The ratios don't align—what is desired and what Christians are providing aren't meeting the needs of a culture waiting to be heard.

By the way, do you know what spiritually curious non-Christians say are the *least* helpful qualities when it comes to discussing faith?

Christians who have all the answers.

Christians who are quick to point out the inconsistencies in other people's perspectives.

Christians who are good at debating topics.

And yet those three so clearly define much of the modern Christian approach to evangelism and evangelism training in our country today.

As my children have grown older, I've thankfully noticed how my parenting style must change along with their development. When they were six years old, a directive parenting style fit well: I would clearly proclaim the truth and what they needed to do. Now that my children are entering their teenage years, I've quickly realized how my parenting communication style needs to shift from directive to drawing them out. I can't just pick up the proverbial hammer and nail some statement down for them like I used to. I need to involve their heart and mind in a conversational process. As I've studied the listening data on evangelism above, I'm wondering if we haven't been approaching non-Christians with a parenting-a-six-year-old style of communication and then wondering why they aren't complying with our direct proclamations.

Are we missing the qualities our changing and spiritually hungry world is longing for?

What if, in order to revive evangelism, we have to move more toward conversation, not just proclamation? What if the skill of listening and spaces to be heard are the missing keys in our post-everything era?

This, I believe, is what makes Alpha (and other listening-based approaches to evangelism) so unique. One of the primary drivers of Alpha's 10-week course is creating a community of people who can absorb questions, allowing the question-asker to get beyond head-level interaction and down into heart-level introspection. After all, it's in that deep place where all of us keep our wounds and longings, needs and desires. And it's at that level where our lives can be transformed.

We do proclaim in an Alpha group, often through the film series or the short talk. The proclamation includes a relevant and gradually unfolding, clear gospel presentation, complete with apologetics and testimonies. But, the bulk of an Alpha evening is a group discussion time where hosts are trained to *not* answer questions. They respond to questions and disagreements with comments like, "Tell me more." Or "That's an interesting perspective, how did you develop that idea? Can anyone else relate?" The Christians are trained to be question askers, not question answerers. We create a space for people to talk out their thoughts, doubts, and questions without seeking to correct them, judge them, or redirect their point of view. The time inevitably comes for people to draw their own conclusions and many, many turn their hearts and lives towards following Jesus.

It's very difficult to access that level of someone's psyche using proclamation alone. Very rarely does a one-way proclamation open up that kind of depth.

This reminds me of something Drew Hyun pointed out when we spoke recently. He said that in Bible college, he and all the other pastors in training took course after course on preaching and teaching. In other words, they were taught to become experts in proclamation—tone, inflection, sermon structure, exegesis, and explanation. But do you know how many courses Christian leaders are required to take during Bible school or seminary that center on learning how to listen?

Not one.

It would be the same for most lay people in the church. We give evangelism training. We teach people the truth and model how to proclaim it. We memorize and regurgitate our stories and statements of faith. We equip people with the knowledge they need to travel all around their town or the internet or the world and share the gospel.

But when do we teach people how to have conversations? When do we teach people how to listen intently?

Again, let me stress: We *should* be trained as pastors and as Christians to proclaim the truth. We do have knowledge that we need and want to convey in a compelling way.

But by neglecting or minimizing the prioritized practice of listening, by not intentionally crafting space for conversation in our lives and in our church evangelism strategies, we're missing the millions of people who will just not show up to our proclamation-only moments.

So, proclaim in your churches, proclaim in your gatherings, proclaim when the Lord leads you to. I'm not trying to dismantle proclamation. But listening is more important than ever. Christians must increasingly become the most effective and equipped listeners on the planet, and by following the way of Jesus, we can. But how?

How to Listen Well

Many of us think we are much better at listening than we actually are; at least, that's true of me. My family has graciously confirmed that time and time again. The first time I led a listening-based group on Alpha some years ago, I realized just how stinking difficult it was! I kept wanting to jump in with an answer or a Bible verse or the five ontological reasons why God exists or a great book recommendation. It's tough to rewire old habits. The problem is that most of the things we think make us good listeners are not necessarily true. In other words, we act in ways to make it *seem* like we are good listeners, and those actions actually show that we're not listening very well.[5]

For example, most people think that in order to be good listeners, there are the three main things they need to do:

- Don't talk while others are speaking.
- Respond to the person who's talking with certain interested facial expressions or verbal sounds that make us sound interested.
- Take in what people are saying and be able to repeat it back to them at the very end.

Wait, you're probably thinking, *That's what I've always been told to do in order to communicate that I'm listening, that I'm paying attention.* But a study on management coaching revealed some surprising things about listening:

Good listening entails a lot more than simply remaining silent while someone else talks. Actually, people label someone a good listener when the listener is asking engaging questions that take the conversation into new areas, questions that show that, not only was the person paying attention, but they're engaged in the conversation and desire additional information.

Good listening builds up the speaker's self-esteem. This can be summed up in one main thought: You will be considered a good listener if, at the end of the conversation, the person doing the talking feels like it was a positive experience. This includes creating a safe space where differences can be talked about, not hidden (one of Alpha's strengths, I might add).

Good listening is experienced as a cooperative conversation. We'll focus on the negative for a moment—people perceived as poor listeners in this study were those who came across as competitive, those who identified errors in reasoning or logic, and those who were obviously using periods of silence to get ready to make their next point. In other words, bad listeners are those who are actually trying to win the conversation.

Good listeners make suggestions. This seems, at first, to be counterintuitive, doesn't it? I've often told myself while listening that I shouldn't be offering up ideas for consideration or further conversation, but it turns out that people who make positive suggestions which flow from a genuinely interested posture are perceived as being good listeners.[6]

David Augsburger writes that, "Being heard is so close to being loved that for the average person they are almost indistinguishable."[7] It is our responsibility as evangelists to diffuse the inflamed discourse of our time. When we reply to deep and complex questions with hard-and-fast answers, we are inadvertently sending messages to the people asking the questions, messages that say:

"I am right, and you are wrong."

"You aren't good enough to have this figured out."

"I have thought this through with wisdom and you have not."

"You aren't accepted in our community because of the way you think."

We can upend those harmful messages and replace them with experienced love by one simple act: listening well. This reminds people they are valued, even in their process of doubt and faith exploration, and that we love them before they believe. If we can do that, if we can be good listeners, people are far more likely to sort out what is true. They might even discover something they're willing to devote the rest of their lives to.

We can't stop there. According to the *Harvard Business Review* article "What Great Listeners Actually Do," there are various levels of listening, each building on the one before it.

Level 1: The listener is able to provide a safe space where hard issues can be talked about.

Level 2: The listener is deliberate about eliminating distractions, things like phones or laptops, and focusing on the other person. Things like eye contact are important at this level of listening.

Level 3: The listener begins responding in a way that illustrates they are seeking to understand. This could include asking questions or being able to summarize what the speaker is talking about.

Level 4: At this level, the listener is not only taking in what the person is saying—they're also paying attention to nonverbal cues and body signals coming their way.

Level 5: The listener begins identifying the feelings and emotions of the speaker, but not only that—they're also empathizing and even validating those feelings even if they don't agree with the premise of what is being shared.

Level 6: The listener is able to ask questions that bring clarification for the listener and the speaker. The listener might even begin interjecting thoughts they have on the topic that are helpful, all the while being careful not to take over the conversation or begin to lead it in another direction.[8]

That's pretty insightful, isn't it? The one that jumps out to me is Level 5. When was the last time you or I had a conversation and, instead of arguing with the other person or trying to change their mind, you listened with the intent of solely validating their feelings on the issue? What impact would that have on the spiritual progress another is making?

That's an entirely new level of conversation.

Listening is one of the most powerful opportunities we have to reduce walls to the gospel: It allows people to be heard; it gives them the rare space to hear themselves as they're speaking; and it hopefully leads to the realization that they are being heard by the God of heaven who loves them.

It is a profound shift, this one that takes us from answering first to listening fully.

The main questions many churches today need to consider are these:

"Are we willing to enter into the slow and free-flowing work of listening? Can we craft spaces for listening within our church culture and church strategies?"

Do we believe verses like Ecclesiastes 3:11 that says, "He has made everything beautiful in its time. He has set eternity in the human heart," implying that God is already at work in someone's heart and life? Do we believe they are created in his image with desire for the divine, and our job is to help them discover what is already embedded within?

We must stop only hammering the truth home from the outside in, treating people's hearts as wooden planks into which we must nail down theological knowledge.

Here are some final, practical ideas to help us grow in this essential skill of listening. These are ways to begin conversations that will draw those who are currently turned off by our history of proclamation alone:

1. *Become curious.* People are so interesting, and yet we can tend to minimize them into a conversion opportunity. It is much easier to authentically ask more questions and facilitate deep conversations when we communicate and embody an approach that says, "I really want to know what you think and who you are."

2. *Ask until asked, and then ask some more.* Often, when I'm hanging out with someone who's not a Christian, I'll ask questions about them until they ask me a genuine question about my faith. I don't lead with declarations—I wait until they ask me a question about me. And, if the question is more intellectual or theological, I'll generally turn it back to them to see what they think. I'm more interested in sharing my story or thoughts when there is an obvious desire for it.

Remember, this was Jesus' approach.

Once they ask me a question that's personal to my own faith experience, then I'll share with them. There's something powerful about waiting until someone wants to hear from you—and some people never get there! At least not in a short period of time. And that's okay.

When it comes to sharing faith, I strongly support the law of supply and demand (concept from the book *Becoming a Contagious Christian*[9]). In other words, when it comes to evangelism, we shouldn't be supplying where there isn't a demand. We can't force feed someone who isn't open to a meal.

Learn how to ask good questions and how to keep asking, and find within yourself a genuine fascination with who people are and how they think.

3. *Affirm.* Just because someone doesn't follow Jesus and adhere to the orthodox convictions of the Christian faith doesn't mean their viewpoints are without any merit. I firmly believe we have much to learn from everyone around us. There is some good we can discover. There is some common ground that can bring us together.

I was once speaking with a friend who deeply distrusts the concept of Biblical authority, which led him to think he couldn't believe in the account of Jesus and his divinity. He was adamant that faith in Christ is unfounded because of how it is based on the account of the resurrection.

But he told me at another point in the conversation how much he loves the mountains and can sense a power and beauty beyond comprehension when he watches the sun set. He was clearly moved by creation and saw something there that could not be explained, and I realized as he was saying this that we shared some common ground.

Rather than initially arguing with the part of his viewpoint I believed to be incorrect, I focused on what I could affirm. "I love your sensitivity to a greater power and presence when you are in nature. That is something many people overlook. You have an ability to see and sense God's presence."

That type of affirmation goes a long way. In time,

there may be moments to further discuss the details of theology or revisit the things we disagree on, but if those conversations are built on foundations of affirmation and commonly held beliefs, they will bear much more fruit.

4. *Learn together.* If the relationship has developed long enough and the spiritual conversations are building, consider reading or watching something together. Books, articles, or films can be some of the best conversation starters, giving you a shared opportunity to ask questions and find out more about what the person believes. Rather than creating a situation where you come across as a know-it-all holding every answer, invite someone to come alongside you as you keep growing. This is also one invitation where activities like the Alpha course provide some help—giving some content like a documentary film about faith that can generate a *learning together* environment.

I remember reading the Gospel of John with many friends who were exploring faith. I shared what I noticed and what was shaping me along the way, and they shared what jumped out to them and what they thought about the text, without me interjecting and correcting. I was introduced to so many new ways of seeing what had become a familiar passage, and more than a few of my friends have become Christians through that process of reading, watching, sharing, and listening—together.

5. *Equip listeners.* Effective training should have as its utmost priority developing and training great listeners. This is Jesus' way. Flip through your latest message on evangelism if you are a pastor. Analyze any evangelism

training courses you're involved with and determine if your messages and courses disproportionately emphasize listening. Remember, Jesus' questions were 40 times more common than his direct answers.

Always be asking yourself how you can encourage the people you are discipling to take on a similar posture and develop the skill of listening.

6. *Provide a space for conversation.* If you are a church leader, think about all the various environments you are creating within your congregation—Sunday mornings, evening classes, online services, small groups, etc. Are they primarily one-directional or primarily for the already convinced? Have you created any spaces within the life of your church for conversation—especially for outsiders—where people with deep doubts, questions, and even hostilities can work out their faith as a conversational journey over time?

You don't need to dismantle the proclamation spaces you've created; God will certainly still use them. But please consider creating an additional space for conversation for the many who won't be reached by proclamation along. By now you can see that I have a strong bias for activities like Alpha groups as a scalable space for conversations which create a new front door in your church for those seeking interaction and not just proclamation.

If you aren't in charge of programs at your church, think about spaces you create for conversation in your daily life with those who don't follow Jesus. Is there enough time in the margins, or enough invitations to a table, or enough engaging moments where you can enter into a listening-based conversation with a spiritually curious someone?

Absorbing Our World's Hostility

A deeply devout atheist showed up at Drew's church for the Alpha course. She held deep convictions about the world and what made it up, how things were ordered, and the compelling nature (in her view) of humanism. She attended the entire course, and you know what happened in the end?

Nothing.

Well, not exactly nothing. She didn't become a Christian. She didn't renounce her view of the world. But she did begin attending Drew's church on a weekly basis.

Why?

Why would an atheist who hadn't come to faith commit to attending weekly religious services?

"She saw that we are normal people who care for each other and are seeking the truth," Drew explained. "She's still on her journey."

But there's something else Alpha allowed to happen in this situation:

"Through Alpha, we've created an environment where we can absorb the hostility of New York," Drew said quietly. "We're learning how to become loving and listening human beings."

This is such a beautiful thing, and I'm proud of my friend Drew for the environment he has created, one where someone who does not believe in God feels comfortable enough to engage in conversation, sharing her views of the world, and becoming friends with people in the church. One day her life in Christ and eternity might change too.

Where do people in your community go when they have questions or doubts?

Have you created an environment that allows for these things, or are people expected to begin wholesale assimilation directly after they show up?

If all we're offering are hand-raising salvation moments or small groups where people sit around and speak in Christianese, then people with doubt will have no place in the church. If all we've been trained to do is proclaim our faith, we're actually causing our culture to build more walls. We will never earn our way into someone's friendship and heart by proclamation alone.

We have to create space for conversation.

What happens when we create space for conversation? A deeper issue emerges which we'll discuss next; something you'll unearth once you are at the table with those not yet following Christ.

What Next?

- How will you create a space for conversation in your church?
- How can you grow at the art of listening?
- When is the last time you had a conversation with someone whom you vehemently disagreed?
- How did it go? Is there anything about that conversation you wish would have been different?

Belonging, Not Just Welcoming

A couple planned to launch a church in downtown Honolulu, situated in an area renowned for painting, photography, acting, and music. It was the artsy epicenter of the city, and they were excited about starting a church in that creative hub.

But they didn't want to simply start a welcoming space. They wanted a community where people felt like they belonged. They wanted to practice radical hospitality to the creatives living and working in that part of the city. As they looked around and saw what was and wasn't working in the church-planting world, they decided their strategy— their entire plan for laying the early foundation of their future church community—was going to be based around putting on great dinner parties.

They didn't think the current evangelism strategies

were working, or at least working enough. They wanted people to feel like they belonged. They didn't want to start a new church service just to fill it up immediately with Christian transfers from surrounding churches. And they didn't think, after many interactions, that the unchurched, artistic community was initially open to attend a Sunday morning meeting where they would sit and listen to one speaker deliver their thoughts.

So, they laid the foundation of their church with dinner parties where the starting aim was simply forming a sense of community and conversation. The effort would grow over time into deep pathways of discipleship and, yes, church services too—but it didn't start there.

These gatherings were well attended. The food and drink were amazing, and as they focused on this objective—creating a fun space with good food that fostered conversation and a sense of community—they began to see more and more young creatives showing up. Models. Actors. Musicians. They were all coming around the table, enjoying each other's company, and building this strong sense of belonging.

There was one woman whom they noticed, a model who joined everyone at the table but seemed to be perched on the outskirts of what was going on. As they paid closer attention, they realized she wasn't eating during the meal. She was listening. At the end of the meal, she would, in a very subtle way, put some food in a small, plastic container and then place the container in her bag and leave with it.

What was going on? Why wasn't she joining in the meal?

The leaders were taken aback by this. One night, they

saw her do it again. At the end of the meal, she very quietly took out her Tupperware container, filled it with food, and slipped the container into her bag.

So, they approached her.

"Look," one of them said in a kind voice. "We actually have plenty of food. In fact, there is so much left over at the end of the night that you're welcome to take as much as you want. Help yourself! We'd love to send more home with you, for you or your roommates or anyone else. If you need more, you can have it—but please don't let that keep you from eating here, with all of us."

The young model smiled and shook her head.

"No, no," she said. "That's not it at all. When I'm here in this place, with these wonderful people you've brought together, I feel so filled up that I don't even need to eat. This experience is enough as it is. I take the food home with me to remember the taste of what it felt like to be honored and loved by you and everyone else here, in this way."

What a beautiful story of someone who found an unexpected sense of belonging, and it all began with a couple who wanted to serve as hosts to others. A host is "one that receives or entertains guests socially, commercially, or officially."[1] When you take on the role of host, your goal is to serve the guest, and for the Christian this cannot only take place in church—we must be hosts to our unbelieving friends and family everywhere in our lives: in our homes, our schools, our parks, our communities, and even online.

What's the real takeaway though from this story of a couple who hosted a meal? That church services and revival meetings aren't what people are looking for? That if you start serving food, good things will happen? That churches need to disband to create time for Sunday evening meals together?

Please hear me: I'm not advocating for the abolition of church services and large group meetings at all. I'm not saying that all churches need to immediately stop what they're doing and figure out how to start dinner clubs. I'm not saying all churches or church plants should become house churches or pub gatherings. Far from it.

But I am suggesting that if we're going to see this new generation of people come to know Jesus in a meaningful way, and if we're going to equip this new generation of Christians with evangelism tools that work, we have to become hosts who are aware of what people are looking for: a sense of belonging.

Welcoming? Or Belonging?

For the last few decades, churches have worked very hard at welcoming those who come in from the outside; cue the "seeker sensitive" shift which began with today's Boomers in the 1970s. We've created slogans that include the phrase, "All are welcome!" and we've hung huge banners throughout our entryways that read "Welcome home!" Some churches offer specific small groups where newcomers are encouraged to attend, and pastors have adjusted the way they speak, dropping a lot of the old church jargon.

We've tried very hard to make our congregations more

welcoming, encouraging regular attenders to be on the lookout for first-time visitors. Be kind. Get to know them. Some churches even train people who sit in the audience every Sunday how to recognize guests and engage them. Recently, this has translated to welcoming chat threads to visitors at our online services.

We say things like:

"Glad to see you."

"Hey, let me know if you need anything."

"Can I get you a coffee?"

"You're always welcome in our church."

When we implement these types of welcoming behaviors, we attempt to make surface-level changes that can help a new person feel less out of place. We let people know what our community expects (sometimes verbally, sometimes nonverbally), but we do it in a kind way that isn't imposing.

From the visitor's or outsider's perspective, they would probably describe a "welcoming" church as nice, friendly, or pleasant. Maybe it reminds them of other, non-church venues like local coffee shops, clothing boutiques, good restaurants, or the DMV (okay, that last one is a stretch).

The people smile a lot.

They were very friendly.

They seemed happy to have me there.

Here's the problem: when a church congregation stops at welcoming and doesn't move into helping people feel a sense of genuine belonging, the experience falls short and becomes diluted.

What we sometimes fail to recognize is that many welcoming environments can actually make people feel very uncomfortable . . . until they, the visitors, make a change. When we're welcoming, we unintentionally communicate that, "Hey, you can sit at our table or in our seats, you can hear my thoughts, you can receive my messages, you can attend my events, and you can enter into this gathering and online space with us . . . on our terms." Welcoming environments can often inadvertently feel like assimilation chambers. We even use that expression—*assimilation*—for some of our strategies, staff roles, and church departments.

There's a natural distance that a welcoming, assimilation-focused environment can unintentionally impose on a discerning, post-everything audience. It's all smiles and kind words and even hot coffee. But, at the end of the day, too many welcoming environments withhold the beyond-the-surface-level-belonging and involvement until the new person figures out what behaviors and beliefs are expected, and they adhere to those. They can never quite feel like they belong . . . until they decide to sign on the dotted line. Or swear off all the old ways. Or speak in the new vernacular.

Don't get me wrong—our churches should be welcoming. When someone walks through those doors for the first time or logs on to that virtual church gathering, it can be very intimidating, so we should work hard to create environments and services that feel warm and inviting. We should smile. We should break the ice with conversation and DMs. We should offer hot coffee. We should be welcoming. We should also desire that people will one day change their beliefs and their behaviors to follow Jesus.

But for too long the Western church hasn't gone further than welcoming, and we're seeing the fruit of that subtle exclusion—eroding evangelism effectiveness, declining church attendance, and greater distance from impacting the lives of those around us.

I love the generosity to outsiders modeled within the Bible, first illustrated in the context of the Old Testament. And it's not the kind of generosity that starts and stops with simply welcoming. Take this command of the Lord from Leviticus 19:34:

> The foreigner residing among you must be treated as your native-born. Love them as yourself, for you were foreigners in Egypt. I am the LORD your God.

Treating someone as a native-born citizen? Loving them as you love yourself? That's not simply welcoming—that's extending a sense of core, communal belonging to an obvious outsider. Think of the religious, cultural, political, and ethnic differences God was asking his people to overcome to create belonging to a non-Hebrew as a native-born citizen! Think of how this may apply within a church or a Christian community context with someone outside the faith: a foreigner, so to speak. God's heart and command is that we treat such a person as a native-born citizen within our faith family.

But why, God? Why this command to create a space of belonging in the midst of your people? Because, he essentially says, you know what it is like to be outsiders. "You were foreigners in Egypt." That's the reason God gives for this call to belonging. Do you remember what it feels like to be on the outside?

The same can be found all through the New Testament as well, with one example in Luke 14:12–14:

> Then Jesus said to his host, "When you give a luncheon or dinner, do not invite your friends, your brothers or sisters, your relatives, or your rich neighbors; if you do, they may invite you back and so you will be repaid. But when you give a banquet, invite the poor, the crippled, the lame, the blind, and you will be blessed. Although they cannot repay you, you will be repaid at the resurrection of the righteous."

How often do we in the church or in our personal lives set the table for outsiders, people in the place of spiritual poverty? Or, have we developed the habit of serving only "insiders" like our friends and family? We work hard to make those we know and love feel like they belong, but what about the outsiders coming in? Are we crafting true spaces of belonging for outsiders in our churches or just "listen-to-what-we-think" spaces for outsiders?

What's most interesting to me is this likely weakness displayed in so many of our churches lines up opposingly with a felt need in young people today. Forty-seven percent of Millennials say they "experience a general sense of emptiness." And a similar percentage say they "often feel rejected."[2]

There is an entire generation of young people yearning to belong.

Being welcoming isn't enough.

People are looking for something else, something more.

And there's nothing that fast-tracks a sense of belonging more effectively than radical hospitality.

When Did We See You?

In one of Jesus' more controversial sermons, he addresses this concept of radical hospitality by bringing those he is teaching into an interesting scenario: the Son of Man has come into his glory, is surrounded by angels, and sits on his throne. It's at this point that all the nations are brought, and he begins to separate them, "as a shepherd separates the sheep from the goats." He carries on this separation until all of the sheep are on his right side and the goats are on his left.

> "Then the King will say to those on his right, 'Come, you who are blessed by my Father; take your inheritance, the kingdom prepared for you since the creation of the world. For I was hungry and you gave me something to eat, I was thirsty and you gave me something to drink, I was a stranger and you invited me in, I needed clothes and you clothed me, I was sick and you looked after me, I was in prison and you came to visit me.'
>
> "Then the righteous will answer him, 'Lord, when did we see you hungry and feed you, or thirsty

and give you something to drink? When did we see you a stranger and invite you in, or needing clothes and clothe you? When did we see you sick or in prison and go to visit you?'

"The King will reply, 'Truly I tell you, whatever you did for one of the least of these brothers and sisters of mine, you did for me.'"

Matthew 25:34–40

Jesus paints a convicting end-times picture, when every nation on earth has gathered before him. It's time for the great judgment, time for Jesus to make a distinction between those who did his will and those who did not. What's interesting is that Jesus doesn't ask them to bring to the throne of grace their church doctrine or their baptismal archives.

He separates the sheep from the goats based on how well they served the outsider, how successful they were in creating spaces of belonging.

"For I was hungry, and you gave me something to eat."

"For I was thirsty, and you gave me something to drink."

"I was a stranger and you invited me in."

"You looked after me."

"You invited me in."

"You visited me."

True, this passage is largely referencing "outsiders" in a state of physical or relational poverty, but doesn't the principle also apply to those under the crushing weight of spiritual poverty as well? We might imply an extension of the text, *I was empty and starving for meaning and purpose and connection to the Creator and you brought me in, you listened, you allowed me to belong.*

Notice the depth and breadth of those actions. These aren't simply "welcoming" actions—shaking hands, saying hello, sending an email, or smiling at someone. This is the kind of radical hospitality that requires something of us, the kind of service that reaches into someone's deepest needs and creates intentional space for them even while they are still "outsiders." These are the kind of actions that might at first feel like an inconvenience, costing us money or time or even reputation. They are not activities we can do as an afterthought or by accident.

Jesus is clear in this passage: What contributes to the kingdom inheritance which God has prepared for us since before the beginning of time?

We serve people, and we create spaces of belonging through radical hospitality.

A Christian couple at New Life Church in Colorado Springs wanted to grow in the practice of radical hospitality. They started out by delivering groceries to a family in need in their community. During the visit they discovered a woman, Tammy, who didn't have a place to stay—she had been sleeping on the couch in the home where they delivered the groceries.

Then they found out she was pregnant with twins.

After prayer and conversation with wise friends, they approached the young woman.

"Why don't you come live with us?" they asked.

"We have a guest room. You're more than welcome to stay there for a little while."

For a few months, she wouldn't go to church with them—she didn't know anything about church. But one Sunday she decided to go along.

As time passed, another church family stepped in because they had even more space with a separate kitchen. Everyone made arrangements for Tammy to move again, and other members of the church threw a baby shower for her, supplying her with a stroller, a crib, and all the other things a new mother might need.

Tammy's boyfriend was in and out of prison. She had relapses with drugs. But her new church community rallied around her. Even though she didn't fully believe or behave as the church members did, Tammy belonged.

The twins were born, and she continued making progress. She showed up at church more regularly. She even got sober, found her own place, started out on her own. Tammy eventually did commit herself to Christ, is growing in faith, and living a healthy life as a single mother.

Radical hospitality leads to a sense of belonging, which in turn opens our eyes to the truth and to transformation.

John Mark Comer tells a different story about belonging. A young man came up to him at his church and said, "Man, I just went through the Alpha course."

"Oh, that's great," John said. "What did you think about it?"

The young man waved his hand dismissively. "Oh, it's total BS." But he didn't elaborate.

"Oh," John said, a little taken aback, but before he could speak, before he could begin to muster up some kind of defense of the material, the young man continued.

"But I absolutely loved being there, and I feel so connected to the group. I'm coming back to the next one, and I'm going to bring some friends with me."

Radical hospitality creates spaces of belonging, and it is in these kinds of spaces that people can let down their defenses and eventually have true encounters with God.

Steps to Belonging

In some ways, the business world has been exploring the idea of belonging for years. It may be more surface level than what we are talking about within the church, but companies do understand the concept that belonging is paramount.

While Starbucks has a wide range of hot and cold drink flavors, customers are paying for more than a cup of coffee. Actually, they are paying for everything but the coffee according to Bryant Simon, a Temple University professor who has studied the Starbucks phenomenon around the world.

Simon has figured out what makes it so appealing.

"Starbucks, through its stores and various mechanisms, created something that was valuable to people," said Simon.

Simon says that Starbucks is able to offer things that make people feel good about themselves in more ways than one. Carrying a Starbucks cup gives a sense of belonging to a special club.[3]

Did you catch that at the end?

"Carrying a Starbucks cup gives a sense of belonging . . ."

Entrepreneur magazine begins to explain this phenomenon in the article, "The Five Emotions that Drive Customer Loyalty." Guess what one of those five emotions are?

That's right.

Belonging.

One of the best ways to ensure customer loyalty is to make your customers feel that they're truly a part of something when they engage with your brand. That something can be as in-depth as a customer-run forum and ongoing community or something smaller like the ability to engage with your blog commenters on an individual basis.

The key is to make customers feel that they belong to your brand, the way others might "belong" to a clique or fit in at work. To do this, you'll need to maintain an approachability, and give customers some level of engagement on an individual basis.

I'm not suggesting that you try to manipulate customers' emotions, or that they even can be directly manipulated. Instead, their needs should be considered the same way you'd consider the emotions of a friend or family member.[4]

That's a powerful statement of awareness: "Their needs should be considered the same way you'd consider the emotions of a friend or family member." Sounds a lot like "treating the foreigner as a native-born citizen." This is just the business community trying to make a buck. How much more important is belonging for the church who is called to offer the eternal help and hope of Jesus Christ?

As we move beyond the creation of welcoming places and into spaces that foster a sense of belonging, let's keep in mind that we can't seek this outcome in manipulative ways. People know when they're being manipulated, and especially this generation of Millennials and even more so among Gen Z. They can spot a fraud a million miles away.

Our culture is increasingly feeling a sense of disconnection and rejection. There is an implicit hunger and need for what belonging can bring with it. The data reveals that Christians have insulated ourselves and aren't creating enough space for outsiders—38 percent of practicing Christian adults say they don't have a single non-Christian friend or family member,[5] and almost half of adult Christians in the US have just 2 or fewer general spiritual conversations a year with non-Christians.[6] And, when outsiders finally make their way into any spaces within our churches or lives, too often we're requiring them to believe like us before they can experience true belonging.

If we as the church can consider the needs of those around us the same way we might be on the lookout to support other church members, friends, or family, then a sense of belonging is just around the corner.

There are some basic, practical things we can do to create spaces where people feel not only a sense of welcome but also of belonging:[7]

Start by showing up. Think about how important it has been when someone has shown up to an event that was important to you—whether your wedding, the launch of your business, the funeral of a loved one, or one of your kids' recitals or competitions. Do you remember how it felt when you saw them coming through the crowd and realized they had taken time out of their busy schedule to attend something important to you?

When we show up, we are telling those involved that they are important to us, that we value them, and, best of all, that they belong in our lives and in our community. People shouldn't always have to come to us or show up in our spaces—we should be willing, even excited, to turn up at other people's big moments and be an encouraging, hospitable presence.

Once we're there, act like a host. My friend Glenn Packiam was involved in planning the funeral for a friend's loved one who had died, but the friend didn't want to host the funeral at a church. They had a lot of acquaintances who weren't believers, and they didn't feel like those folks would be very comfortable attending in a place of worship. So, they held the funeral at a neutral location and didn't involve Glenn or any of the other pastors from the church during the event.

It would have been very easy for Glenn to sit in the service and feel awkward about not being invited to officiate the funeral. He could have mulled over all the ways his church had served this family—why wouldn't they just have the funeral in the sanctuary? He could have quickly left at the conclusion of the service; after all, they hadn't given him any formal responsibility, so maybe he should just bail?

But Glenn didn't take any of those options. He decided he was going to connect with people in the room as if he was the host. He switched his mindset, realizing he was in their space at the most difficult time of their lives, and others had gathered with them. It wasn't his space, but he could still provide an intentional hospitable presence to those who were there.

When we are willing to engage in spaces that aren't ours, we create arenas of belonging.

Leave space in our lives. As we mentioned earlier, Barna data has revealed that 38 percent of practicing Christians say that all of their friends are Christians. We don't have to judge church people for not having non-Christian friends—it's simply the double-edged sword of having a good community at church where you feel like you belong (and ambitiously active lifestyles). Once you create belonging with other Christians, that becomes your community, and they become your people.

But as Christians we have to leave space in our lives to make sure we are entering into places with people who aren't like us. Glenn coached his son's soccer team for four years and realized pretty quickly that he didn't know at least half of the families—they don't go to church, and he, like most pastors, finds it hard to make time to go into unchurched settings. He's known when he's standing at the pulpit. He's recognized in the coffee shops and restaurants where he meets with church people.

But in the community? Not so much.

We have to make sure we're not making decisions that wholly insulate us, and we have to start looking for opportunities that send us out into an unfamiliar world . . . where we can show up for non-Christian friends and play the role of a kind host.

Break bread. When it comes to radical hospitality and creating spaces of belonging, there are few activities as effective as sitting around a table and sharing a meal.

We go to the fast food drive-through on our way to evening activities. We grab a quick bowl of cereal on our way out the door in the morning. We wolf down our lunch at work in those fifteen precious minutes.

And yet, even though we're all eating multiple times a day, so few of us deliberately sit down around a table and share a meal together.

But there's something powerful about that decision, because when we eat with someone else, we slow down. We pause the hectic rhythm of life, we breathe, and we look into each other's eyes again.

It's made even more meaningful when you prepare the meal together.

That's one of the reasons people at New Life Church decided to do meal groups and then beyond those meal groups, the Alpha course—it's a time for all of them at the church to press pause, to face forward, to listen to someone as they're talking. These are all necessary things when it comes to creating meaningful relationships. And relationships are the primary driver when it comes to making someone feel like they belong.

Is it still great to do Bible studies and small group studies? Of course. Those are effective and necessary. Those are primarily for insiders though.

The picture of the kingdom Jesus often paints looks more like a table than a temple. And, Jesus often accomplished more ministry around a table than in the temple. Again, I'm not trying to discount the power and essential need of large gatherings in church every week. But, when Jesus was ministering to outsiders or describing the kingdom of heaven, the picture is of a banquet where outsiders are invited to come and feast with the king, the master, in lavishness. In these parables and in his own moments around a table, those who attend are meant to be there. They were invited. They belonged.

Jesus envisions a kingdom that includes total generosity to outsiders which requires spaces intentionally created for outsiders.

Come to Me

Creating spaces of belonging doesn't come without its challenges.

Many Christians might wonder, "Wait a minute. How can we move beyond 'welcome' and help people feel a sense of belonging if they're living in certain ways, engaging in sin, or have completely different worldviews than we do?" It's a good question. It's a hard question. And trying to create spaces of belonging will lead to tension and difficult conversations.

But living life and attending church or participating in a meal gathering or the Alpha course alongside people we disagree with is a powerful evangelistic tool. If people can feel like they belong, if they can be drawn into the relationships and love that we have for each other, they will be drawn closer to Christ. And that's when we begin to treat each other like friends.

Friends are going to show up with meals for you in hard times.

Friends, no matter your beliefs, will visit you in the hospital, attend the funeral of a loved one, or come to your children's activities.

Friends, no matter the worldview, will eat with you and share their life and time with you.

Make no mistake—biblical, radical hospitality will cost something, because it means we are willing to create spaces and times and gatherings that aren't only about us or about those we're comfortable with.

If you're a pastor, initially this kind of belonging might cost you parishioners.

If you're a lay person, creating spaces of belonging might make other Christians wonder what you really believe.

It might cost some reputation with insiders.

But not everything we do or invest in is for the sake

of the church members. It simply can't be. Actually, the church should be the only institution on the planet that exists for the benefit of its non-members.

Just look at the ministry of Christ. He sat around the table with people who were notorious sinners, and he even invited his disciples to journey with him long before they declared he was the Messiah. He was known as their friend. Consider Peter—Jesus ate with him, went to his mother-in-law's house, traveled with him, and created a space where Peter belonged long before Peter's recorded confession of faith.

How many potential disciples have we turned away because we're not willing to create spaces of belonging that are available before belief occurs?

We must create space for those on the outside, places where outsiders can belong.

We are called to a high bar of radical hospitality.

When people taste belonging it reveals a longing for so much more. Dive into the following pages with me to unpack our next catalytic shift.

What Next?

- Do I currently believe the best and only strategy for evangelism is to get people into the temple, the church?
- How can I incorporate more table time with those outside the church into my personal life?
- What are things others do for me that feel like radical hospitality?

Experience, Not Just Explanation

Not long ago, a married woman started attending a MOPS (Mothers of Preschoolers) group held at a church, and she started thinking about what life with God might look like. After a couple of months spending time with other women in the group, she began attending that church. She attended every Sunday, and she brought her children with her. Every week she went home from church and told her husband that he should come along with her next time. (MOPS, by the way, does a phenomenal job at creating spaces for conversation and belonging around a table which we've discussed—I'm a huge fan!)

The woman's husband (we'll call him Allen) didn't have much spare time or interest in spiritual matters. But she kept inviting him, so, like a good engineer, he checked out the church online. He browsed their activities and scrolled their leadership page, looking to see who the pastor was. After exploring whatever he could find out about the church on the internet, he eventually thought, *Well, they don't seem entirely crazy.*

So, he attended church with his wife one Sunday. Then he started going with her every few weeks. It became part of their routine, and soon they were going to church together almost every week.

Allen was very logical, very cerebral. He owned his own company, and he talked and thought like an engineer. He started attending church every week. That's when he heard about Alpha, and something about the straightforwardness of it, the logical progression, appealed to him. He thought it might be interesting to analyze this spiritual stuff in a little more detail, so he signed up. He attended Alpha every single week, looking forward to the conversations and categorizing in his mind everything he learned.

And every single week, after their time together at Alpha ended, he asked the pastor for additional resources. If they talked about church history, he asked for the best book on it. If they discussed the Trinity, he wanted another book or video or article. Every week, he was reading books, thinking more and more about the material, and coming to his own conclusions. He even surprised himself by how interested he was in the Christian faith and how much time he was spending on research.

This all led to Alpha's weekend away, when everyone spends some extended time together thinking deeply about God and being introduced to prayer and the Holy Spirit.

Allen decided he wanted to go along. He approached his pastor, Jay, just before Jay was about to give the opening talk of the weekend.

Allen told Jay he *knew* what was going on. He could tell the crescendo was coming, that Jay was probably going to try to make him do something he didn't want to do, something based completely out of emotion. Allen thought a lot of what happened in religious environments was based more on manipulation and suggestion than reality.

"That's not true at all," Jay said. "There's no manipulation coming for you this weekend, Allen. And please don't do anything you don't want to do. That's not why we came on this retreat."

Allen looked skeptical.

"I'm serious," Jay said. "No shouting, no special music. We're not going to dim the lights or pull on your heart strings. Nothing like that. We're just going to teach you about the Holy Spirit and give you a chance to pray."

"Okay," Allen said, but there was still skepticism in his voice. He joined the group for that particular teaching.

Jay presented the Alpha material on how to experience God's presence. "If you want someone to pray with you, if you want to have an experience with God, stand up, right where you are, and one of us will come and pray with you."

Allen stood up.

"Why are you standing?" Jay asked, a little confused. Wasn't this the guy who was skeptical about everything?

"I'm already here," Allen explained, shrugging. "If this stuff you're talking about is true, then it's worth trying."

"Okay." Jay walked to where Allen was standing and very simply put his hand on Allen's shoulder and prayed quietly, "Allen, be filled with the Holy Spirit."

After a few moments of quietly waiting, Allen doubled over and started weeping deep, heart-wrenching tears from the center of his being. He cried and cried, completely overcome.

Later that day, Allen found Jay and pulled him aside. "Jay, this stuff is real."

Jay smiled. "Yeah, I know it is."

"No," Allen repeated. "This stuff is real. Like gravity is real."

"Yeah," Jay said, laughing this time. "I know it's real. As real as gravity."

Something had shifted in Allen. He went from contemplating a philosophy to encountering a reality. Allen had given himself fully to Jesus and his heart and life began to change even more after that one experience.

He went from seeking an explanation about God to experiencing God.

And his journey didn't stop there.

The Gospel Is . . . What?

I remember leading evangelism and outreach efforts in two large churches, and I also remember looking at the results of those outreaches, scratching my head the entire time. Were those numbers correct? The honest truth was the results were much lower than any of us had desired. It didn't seem like anything we were doing was working particularly well, and no matter how confident we were with a program or outreach, no matter how much money we spent, the results never lived up to our hopes.

Why weren't more people coming to know Jesus?

Why weren't those who came forward or raised their hands to follow Jesus coming back to church?

Was the transformation simply not sticking?

It was disappointing and frustrating. We worked hard, we strategized, and we even executed the plans we created, but nothing was quite as fruitful as we would have liked.

One day, I read Romans 1:16 with fresh eyes, and the floor dropped out from under me:

> For I am not ashamed of the gospel, because it is the power of God that brings salvation to everyone who believes . . .

I sat and stared at the text for a few minutes, rereading that verse over and over again.

Has that ever happened to you? Have you ever read a Bible verse many times in your life but then you read it once more and it becomes saturated with new meaning?

Being completely honest with myself, if I looked at how I used my time and my energy toward evangelism, I was living and leading and training others as if the gospel, the good news, was the *explanation of man* for the salvation of those who believed. Or maybe I was living as if the gospel was *the strategy of the church and my efforts to be productive* for the salvation of those who believe.

But that's not what the verse says.

It says, the gospel "is the power of God that brings salvation to everyone who believes."

The power of God.

This convicting moment was reminiscent of one described by John Wimber (founder of the Vineyard movement), when he heard the Lord speak to him in 1976. "I've seen your ministry, John. Now I'm going to show you mine."[1]

Holy Spirit mic drop.

Here's the problem: Most of my evangelism efforts in those days were my attempts to lead people into the gospel through an explanation of God rather than both an explanation and an experience of God. Then I wondered why I wasn't seeing the kingdom fruit of greater and greater salvations which held on in a lasting measure. I was acting as if the key was people knowing enough *about* the gospel—I seemed to believe and lead as if the gospel could be fully understood and internalized through explanation alone.

I realized I needed to depend more on the power of God, the experience of God, especially when it comes to evangelism.

Leading people into an experience with God is one of the bedrocks of Alpha—it is a process and a container that allows people, through listening and conversation, through belonging, through building trust, and through time, to strip away every barrier, arriving at a place where they can finally experience God for themselves. Not just an explanation about him. Not only statements of faith, apologetics, or sound doctrine (all of which are important and all of which are included in Alpha).

That is what we are always trying to do in evangelism: introduce people not just to a theology or doctrine, not just to a religion or a system of beliefs, but into a relationship of experienced love and felt grace and transforming power, in the here and now.

In our *Reviving Evangelism* study with Barna, we found that one of the highest factors reported by non-Christians which would increase their interest in faith was if they "had an eye-opening spiritual experience" themselves.[2] People long for that. They long to feel a connection with the ultimate power who created them, who has a purpose for them, who loves them.

Unfortunately, we've often reduced our evangelism efforts to a cerebral assent when the true power of evangelism comes from an introduction to the Holy Spirit of God. Evangelism is not only an exchange of information; evangelism must become an invitation to God's presence. The deep, spiritual hunger in our world today is for so much more than explanation alone. The hunger is for an experience.

Jesus' Story

Remember the passage from Luke 5 we discussed in the introduction, when Jesus told the tired disciples to go back out into the water and cast their nets once more? There's a section (verses 8–11) I want to revisit with you:

When Simon Peter saw this, he fell at Jesus' knees and said, "Go away from me, Lord; I am a sinful man!" For he and all his companions were astonished at the catch of fish they had taken, and so were James and John, the sons of Zebedee, Simon's partners.

Then Jesus said to Simon, "Don't be afraid; from now on you will fish for people." So they pulled their boats up on shore, left everything and followed him.

This is directly after they bring in that massive haul of fish. Peter sees the miracle and has what appears to be a supernatural revelation of who Jesus is, because he begs Jesus to go away from him. "I am a sinful man!" he cries out.

It was clearly a miraculous event.

It was clearly a show of God's power.

And this experience of God caused four things to happen. First, Peter worships Jesus. He worships! He falls at Jesus' knees because he realizes he has just seen something extraordinary, some supernatural outpouring, and this man, this Jesus, has something to do with it. Something is going on here.

Second, Peter confesses. In his words, we find someone who believes he is not worthy to be in the same place as Jesus. In this way, the gospel was the power of God, and it was bringing salvation to Peter.

Third, Jesus gives Peter a new identity—in the wake of his most successful cast ever, Peter will no longer fish for fish. This was his last hurrah, his final appearance. From now on, Jesus tells him, "You will fish for people."

What an incredible transformation! These are the kinds of transformations we see all the time in Alpha, when people have this kind of a first-person experience of God.

Finally, Peter follows. He leaves everything—everything—and follows Jesus. The other disciples who were present were so amazed by the power they had seen that they, like Peter, pulled their boats up onto the shore and followed Jesus.

Check out another example in Mark 5. Jesus and his disciples get out of a boat after crossing a lake into the region of the Gerasenes. Immediately, a man emerged from the tombs—this was a man with "an impure spirit" who could no longer be bound. He could even break out of chains and iron shackles. He was known in the area because he cried out night and day, and he cut himself with rocks.

He approached Jesus, fell to his knees, and shouted,

> "What do you want with me, Jesus, Son of the Most High God? In God's name don't torture me!" For Jesus had said to him, "Come out of this man, you impure spirit!"
>
> Then Jesus asked him, "What is your name?"
>
> "My name is Legion," he replied, "for we are many." And he begged Jesus again and again not to send them out of the area. (vv. 7–10)

Jesus decides to cast out the evil which had taken up residence in this man into a herd of pigs, and the pigs run over a cliff.

Those tending the pigs ran off and reported this in the town and countryside, and the people went out to see what had happened. When they came to Jesus, they saw the man who had been possessed by the legion of demons, sitting there, dressed and in his right mind; and they were afraid. Those who had seen it told the people what had happened to the demon-possessed man—and told about the pigs as well. Then the people began to plead with Jesus to leave their region. (vv. 14–17)

There are so many amazing things going on in this passage when it comes to having a firsthand experience with God. First and most incredible of all, this man was freed from his affliction. He went from crying out day and night, being the object of scorn and fear, and self-harm, to sitting quietly, dressed, and in his right mind.

The power of God, his experience of God, had set him free.

But this man's experience of God didn't only change him.

As Jesus was getting into the boat, the man who had been demon-possessed begged to go with him. Jesus did not let him, but said, "Go home to your own people and tell them how much the Lord has done for you, and how he has had mercy on you." So the man went away and began to tell in the Decapolis how much Jesus had done for him. And all the people were amazed. (vv. 18–20)

As Jesus was leaving, the man begged Jesus to let him go along. He had experienced Jesus, and he didn't want to part from him. But Jesus tells him to go back to where he came from, back to his own people, and basically be one of Jesus' first missionaries.

And this man's experience with Jesus led him to do just that—he went to the Decapolis and told everyone how much Jesus had accomplished in his life, all the ways Jesus had changed him.

"And all the people were amazed."

Do you see how genuine experiences with God continue radiating out and out, farther and farther, impacting more and more people?

When we lead people into spaces where they can experience God, we aren't only unleashing the power of God in their lives—God will begin to move out from them, to their friends, their family, their neighbors. It's like a rock tossed into the middle of a pond, and the ripples spread outward, reaching all the way to the farthest bank.

How to Facilitate Life-Changing Encounters with God

I can't even count how many times I've sat in an Alpha group while someone has said they *won't believe in a God who allows all the pain and suffering in the world*. How could God allow good people to die from cancer or COVID-19 or be overtaken by mental illness or be swept away by a tsunami? What about all the children who are exploited or die young? What about the people who are trafficked into labor or the sex industry?

What kind of a God would let all of that happen?

And then I see the weeks slide past, and this person begins to process. They experience the kind of belonging that only a loving group of people can bring, and their heart begins to soften. I realize, as they finally share their story, that often at the heart of this anger and confusion is deep pain. Maybe they lost a parent or a sibling or a close friend or are exasperated by this world.

Yes, there are explanations and also accurate theology to undergird our understanding of suffering. Yet, in the midst of that pain, there is no explanation that can transform their mind and heart—only the Spirit of the Lord can do that. But because they've been drawing closer, and because they feel a sense of belonging, and because their heart has started to soften, when we introduce them to prayer and they pray, "I don't yet have this all figured out, but here goes, come, Holy Spirit," it actually works. They experience God. And everything changes.

It was this way with my police officer friend Jason, who, at the scene of a national news tragedy, held innocent, dying people after they were gunned down. Reflecting on that moment in his life, Jason said, "There is no way a good God would allow this." He came to Alpha and prayed with a hardened (but slowly softening) heart full of doubt and suspicion, "God, if you are real, show up," and God did show up. Jason started weeping, let go of his bitterness and hurt, and after being prayed over, said, "I love Jesus. I have no idea how this has happened. My questions aren't even fully answered, but the stone around my heart is gone and love poured in!"

It was this way with Matt, a successful business leader who, after saying yes to Jesus in a time of prayer, experienced his anxiety just disappear. Matt said he felt as if a new chamber in his lungs opened up for the first, deep, anxiety-free breath of air he had taken in his life.

If we want evangelism to revive, we must move away from relying on explanation alone and lead people into a space where they can experience God.

So, what are a few of the keys to blending experience with explanation? What can we do in order to facilitate these kinds of life-changing encounters with God? Here are some ideas:[3]

Ask yourself a fundamental question. This topic brings us back to the question I asked in the "Hunger for More" chapter of this book. You can't take people to places you've never been, so the question is, "Do you regularly have experiences with the living God?" And if not, why not? If we want to introduce our friends or fellow church goers to experiences with God . . . then we have to experience God ourselves. The kingdom is here! The kingdom is among us! We should all be experiencing the presence and power of the Spirit.

When my concern for my son led me to seek more earnestly for God than I ever had before, my experiences of God increased, and eventually my son experienced him as well. So, as you think about those you want to help experience God, first turn your gaze inward and ask what the next step is on your own journey with God.

Where is God already at work? If you want to introduce others toward experiencing God, it's important to stop and think about how God is already at work in you and through you and around you, in the places you already are. Your job in facilitating experiences with God isn't to get people to do certain things or be a certain way—your responsibility includes getting them to see what is already there.

This is one reason Alpha seems to be effective—the course leads people to take baby steps on their spiritual journey, and with each step they're looking for God, not in some far-off place, but in the world around them. Their conversations with the other Alpha attendees, their growing interest in the Bible, and how they begin to pay closer attention to the needs of those around them all help them to begin to see that they can experience God at any time through the people and events right there in front of them.

Listen and pay attention. You "put your hand to it" by listening and paying attention. Once you stop looking for God somewhere "out there" and realize he is working, moving, and acting in you and where you are, the way to come into alignment with that movement is to stop. Listen. Pay attention.

Paying attention might mean having a heart-to-heart conversation with your child or spouse. It might mean finally getting to know the name of your neighbor. It might mean coaching your child's sports team or volunteering at their school or attending a PTA meeting. It might mean going to an AA meeting with your friend or finally calling that aunt or uncle you haven't spoken to in years. Listen to the places the Spirit within you is leading. Pay attention to the life going on all around you.

Pray. Once you start listening and paying attention, prayer is the next logical step. Ultimately, to make it completely practical, experiencing God involves praying. If you believe praying is talking to the God of the universe and having him actually respond to you, then start praying about the places you are and the people who are with you. And above all, ask for eyes to see. Once you start doing this, everything will feel like it's coming much easier.

If you want to see how prayer can be the launching point into the stratosphere of experiencing God, look no further than Jon Tyson and his church from the "Hunger for More" chapter. A dedication to prayer has transformed their congregation, focused their vision, and created opportunities for those outside the church to experience God.

Prayer works.

Create space for God to show up. At some point in an evangelistic process we have to say, "You may not get all these questions and doubts answered, but if God *is* real, he *will* show up. Why don't we ask God to show up and see what happens?" That is a cliff-hanging moment. We might think to ourselves, *What if nothing happens, what if God doesn't show up?* We like to say, "Alpha is perfectly designed to fail, unless God shows up." Because it *is* perfectly designed to fail. It's filled with explanation and conversation and belonging and radical hospitality, but we are ultimately waiting for the power of God alone to lead people to salvation. Shouldn't that be true of all our evangelism efforts, that they are perfectly designed to fail unless God shows up? The ultimate evangelist in every interaction is the Holy Spirit himself: We must create physical and conversational space in our church strategies and evangelism efforts, bringing people to that cliff's edge where God must show up. If not, all we have is a bunch of good human intentions.

A Life Transformed

Remember Allen, the engineer at Jay's church, who experienced God so deeply he gave his life to Jesus Christ? Now, he brings his friends to church, along with his entire family, and they attend every week. After a recent talk Jay gave on giving, Allen came to the front of the church.

"If 10 percent is the minimum standard," Allen said thoughtfully to Jay, "I don't want to just give the minimum. We'll give 15 percent. I'm not sure where that money is going to come from, but we'll go home and look at the budget and figure it out." (The crucial point here isn't about money, it's about the full devotion and heart surrender that materialized in Allen, he wanted *all* for Jesus.)

Allen had been in church for months before that transforming moment at Alpha, during which he had heard a lot of explanations—about the Bible, about the church, about God. And those explanations are all important.

But it wasn't until he experienced God for himself

that his life transformed. It was the experience of God that helped all the knowledge to finally make sense, to click into place, to start the ripple effect into motion.

Jay Pathak, the pastor who led Allen into this experience of God through Alpha, is the lead pastor of a family of five neighborhood churches just outside of Denver. During the last handful of years, they have baptized more than 1,000 people, and they are always doing small surveys and questionnaires to follow up with those who are baptized or saved or go through Alpha.

One of the interesting bits of information they've collected is that somewhere around 70 percent of those who have decided to follow Jesus had some kind of a supernatural experience that moved them over the line, leading them to make that decision.

"We've seen that to be true in Alpha as well," Jay said. "The people who attend are thinking, processing, and opening their hearts to different ways of considering who Jesus is, and this helps them to move beyond obstacles they've run into in the Scriptures and within their lives. The Alpha weekend retreat gives them an opportunity to create a little space that's not hyped up or contrived, a place where they can invite God to speak to them directly. And the amount of people who have some kind of encounter with God is astounding."

Explanation is important. Logic and reason and learning about the truth is essential. But those efforts cannot stand on their own because the gospel is the power of God for the salvation of those who believe.

Momentary encounters with the living God can alter a person in an instant. Yet, there are still barriers, which we'll discuss, that prevent people from opening up in the first place. Let's look at one of those barriers now.

What Next?

* Have you had an eye-opening experience of the Spirit of God? What contributed to that moment? What helped open your eyes?
* Do you think the non-Christians in your life are open to an experience or just an explanation? What is a next step you can take to explore that question with them?
* Does your church create space for people outside the faith to have an eye-opening experience of God's presence as part of their journey toward Christ?

Fruitful, Not Just Factual

Years ago, Kevin and Andrew Palau and their father Luis were preparing for a festival in the city of Portland, a celebration that was a year away and would take place at Waterfront Park. They planned the gathering in the park to celebrate their community, meet tangible needs, and to share the radical, transforming good news of the gospel of Jesus Christ. Kevin, Andrew, and Luis were commissioned by a group of pastors who wanted to begin a relationship with the mayor of Portland, and while they thought the timing was good, they had no idea how this attempt to connect would be received.

The mayor of Portland at the time, Sam Adams, was openly gay and had very negative experiences with the Christian community throughout his life. He lumped most Christians with the aggressive, angry, and overtly harsh judgment he had seen over the years. Partnering with the church certainly seemed like one of the last things on earth this mayor would be interested in, and for good reason. Why join up with a group that never had anything good to say about you, a group that seemed to despise you?

Yet, Kevin and his father wanted to meet with him.

How would they be received by Mayor Adams?

First, I should tell you that my friend Kevin Palau has been working with his dad, the well-known evangelist, Luis Palau, for 34 years. He has spent almost his entire life trying to figure out the best ways for the good news to be proclaimed.

People ask him all the time, "Why in the world are you still in Portland? Your ministry is about supporting churches, so why are you based in one of the least-churched cities in America?"

"It's true," he replies. "Many people actually move to Portland because they know the culture there and they're actively trying to get away from conservative Christians. But in Jeremiah 29:7, God says, 'Also, seek the peace and prosperity of the city to which I have carried you into exile. Pray to the LORD for it, because if it prospers, you too will prosper.' God didn't tell his people, even when they were in exile, to step back and protect themselves and wait for deliverance. He didn't say to fight the culture and somehow take it over. The message he gave was neither of those. The message he gave was to seek the peace and prosperity of the city. So that's what we're trying to do in Portland. That's what we're trying to help churches do in their cities all over the country."

And that's what they were seeking when they walked into the mayor's office with a plan that they hoped would make the church in Portland one of the most fruitful in the country.

Kevin thought it admirable, considering the mayor's prior experience with the church, that he was willing to meet with them, not really knowing what the meeting was going to be about. But Kevin, Andrew, and Luis started off seeking to bring down any barriers that might exist because, as it turns out, they weren't only there to talk about their desired outreach and celebration at the park.[1]

"Mayor Adams," Kevin said, "We love you. Thank you for serving our community. We realize, sadly, that we as a church are known more for what we're against than what we're for, and we want to change that."

They could see Mayor Adams' body shift into a slightly more relaxed position.

"What if we could mobilize 15,000 Jesus followers from churches in the Portland community to partner with you? We would love to serve you and serve the city. And then, one year from now, we'd like to have a celebration in Waterfront Park to gather together. Dad is going to share the message of Jesus and we'll celebrate."

The Palaus, and the churches in Portland, wanted desperately to serve the community, no strings attached. Why? Because they knew their efforts would be fruitful—bringing about improved conditions, a better city, and changed lives. There were so many ways that the lives of people in Portland could be better—poverty needed to be addressed, working families needed support, and the foster care system was overwhelmed. The city faced a lot of challenges.

At first the mayor sat there in silence, not sure what to say. As they talked more about what they had to offer, Kevin could tell the mayor was seriously considering it, and eventually he nodded his head. Yes, he did know of a few ways the church could contribute to the peace and prosperity of Portland. In fact, there was one pressing need they had: the public education system.

The public schools had been one of the reasons Mayor Adams had been elected—he had run for election as an education mayor, promising to address the abysmal state of Portland's city schools—only 55 percent of students in those days were graduating on time. He had promised to turn that around, and with the Palau's offer, it seemed like that might be a good way to test out a partnership between the churches and the city.

Their conversation became more detailed, and Mayor Adams mentioned Roosevelt High School as being one of their schools in particular need. It had been built in the 1920s to serve 2,200 students, but admission had dwindled due to poor community resources over the ensuing decades; now only around 450 kids attended. They had no football team because the grandstands had been condemned as unsafe. The children who attended had a lot of practical needs.

"Help our schools in general," Mayor Adams said. "That would be great, and I can give you some direction on that. But if you could do something for Roosevelt, anything, that would be awesome." He promised to connect them with the superintendent of schools.

In hindsight, Kevin suspects that one of the reasons the mayor (along with the superintendent of schools, a leading figure in the LGBTQ community in Portland) put Roosevelt forward was that they were actually in the beginning stages of closing the school.

"They figured, what harm could these Christians really do?" Kevin said recently, smiling. "'The school will probably be closed soon anyway. Let these Christians give it their best shot.' Well, one church in particular took them up on the offer and got involved—a church called South Lake. They partnered up with Roosevelt, and they gave it their best shot."

The church in Portland was determined to be seen as fruitful in the community. So much so that they were willing to work with anyone in order to serve their community, do good works, and see the gospel message get out to their neighbors.

But this was a tall order. Could their involvement bring attention to, and help turn around, a failing school?

Could their efforts in Portland cause the church to be more fruitful?

They were willing to give it a try.

The Tide of Disinterest

In case you haven't noticed, the church in America doesn't have a great reputation. Just open up your internet browser and begin the search, "Why is the church so . . . ," and you'll see how autofill finishes the question for you after so many searches have already been entered.

"Why is the church so . . . rich?"

"Why is the church so . . . powerless today?"

"Why is the church so . . . silent?"

These are the searches that millions of people across the United States are looking up in Google every single day. Questions that people have about why the church isn't what they wished it would be. There are few people asking, "Why is the church so kind?" or, "Why is the church so giving?" The fact is most people no longer have a positive view of the church.

This alone is an indictment of what we are doing, or not doing, in the western church.

It wasn't always this way. Christianity used to be known as fruitful. The community used to turn to churches and religious organizations to help solve the social problems of the day or to provide for them when times of great need came along. The church used to be the center of the community.

But things changed, and as time passed the prevailing attitude toward the church shifted to being acceptable. In other words, if you were a Christian, that was okay— people didn't see it as being necessarily a positive, but they weren't concerned about it. The church was seen as neutral.

But the shift didn't stop there. Soon people began to be a little more skeptical—if the church is your kind of thing, people wondered about you. They heard of the sex scandals and the financial mismanagement and greed of prominent evangelists. A growing antagonism toward not only the church but people of faith took root. Today, in the wider culture, Christians and the church are perceived not only as irrelevant or ineffective but as extremist and part of the problem. People often stereotype the church as negligent regarding social problems, or worse, the primary source of division and pain and perpetuated intolerant aggression in society. And it's not entirely unfounded. The church often fails to live up to her own standards. When non-Christians think of the church, they often default to thinking of judgmental and hypocritical people, negative and controlling environments, broken relationships and power-mongering, walking by the under-resourced and broken in our world.

If you grew up in the church and you had a largely positive experience, this might be difficult to believe. Or if you live in an area of the country where a large percentage of people still go to church, this progression might be difficult for you to accept.

But the *Reviving Evangelism* study touches on some of these issues. Of the non-Christians and lapsed Christians surveyed, they said that only 34 percent of the Christians they know personally listen without judgment. Only 17 percent demonstrate interest in other peoples' stories or lives. And only 20 percent of the Christians they know personally take the time to know the story of the person they're sharing their faith with.[2]

Although it is heartbreaking, maybe this relatively new view of the church isn't that far off base. Maybe it's not the result of a liberal media or fringe government officials, but of our own, very real failings.

Traditionally, how have we tried to counteract that growing cultural belief that the church is harmful, judgmental, and disinterested in anything but your conversion?

Usually, we just keep pounding the truth.

We just keep preaching.

We just keep reiterating the facts.

Our evangelism efforts, for quite some time now, have focused on making sure everyone knows Christianity is true, along with the fact that what others believe is wrong. In the face of people who think Christianity is harmful, our reply is to accentuate the facts even louder—Christ existed, lived, and died for all of us to be saved. Here is the correct theology. Here is the right moral stance.

We are quick to point out where others fall short and are less interested in their point of view.

And we still need to share the truth—hear me out here. I bless that truth side of the equation. But if we open our eyes and are honest with ourselves, people are not *only* doubting whether or not what we're saying is true.

What they're doubting is whether or not it's *good*, whether or not Jesus followers are good.

Is Christianity actually good for my life?

Is Christianity actually good for society?

Does Christianity lead to changed people who do good works?

Or does it lead to hateful, judgmental hypocrites?

We have a lot of reputation (and heart) work to do.

Before we can effectively convince people today that following Jesus is factual, we have to also show them that following Jesus is fruitful.

There are some other interesting data points about what people out there are really looking for. In the *Reviving Evangelism* study, we also discover that seven in ten non-Christians and lapsed Christian adults are not on a self-prescribed quest for spiritual truth. Seven in ten.[3] That means that most people, even when presented with compelling facts, aren't initially interested in them.

Facts simply are not always the right starting point.

Thirty-eight percent of the same group reports they "don't have any questions about faith." Of course, this percentage is higher among the atheists and agnostics in the group, but over a third are saying they don't have questions . . . so why do we keep trying to give them answers to questions they're not asking?

But 34 percent, or one-third of non-Christians, do hint at something that might raise their interest in following Jesus. There is something we as the church could do to begin flipping the equation.

What might that be?

Reputation. One-third of non-Christians have said they would actually be interested in the Christian faith . . . if Christianity had a better reputation.[4] This is one of the highest reported factors compared to any other that would open their heart to faith.

What we are seeing is an entire group of people who aren't looking for the facts we have, who have few if any questions about the faith, but *will* become interested if the church can somehow salvage its reputation. They would be interested . . . if the church did more good. If the church stopped fighting among itself. If the people in the church could, as a top priority, make positive changes in the world.

And yet we keep trying to bring people to faith by using facts alone. By talking about truth. By making philosophical arguments.

What if there's another, more effective way?

What if our fruitfulness could turn this tide of disinterest?

But the fruit of the Spirit is love, joy, peace, forbearance, kindness, goodness, faithfulness, gentleness and self-control. Against such things there is no law.

Galatians 5:22–23

Reawakening Curiosity

Jesus was the perfect balance of factual and fruitful. He gave us the awe-inspiring Sermon on the Mount, he taught in the synagogues, and he seemed to spend a fair amount of time explaining his teachings to his disciples. Jesus was definitely a conveyor of facts and truth.

But he didn't leave it at that. He didn't simply preach and go home.

Jesus' ministry was also very fruitful, and the direct effect of those good works was that more people found him and decided to follow him. He was constantly ministering to those who were hurting, healing those who were sick, and giving hope to the downtrodden and marginalized.

What if the church became more like Jesus in this way?

Consider the story from John 6, where Jesus was being followed by a large crowd.

> Sometime after this, Jesus crossed to the far shore of the Sea of Galilee (that is, the Sea of Tiberias), and a great crowd of people followed him because they saw the signs he had performed by healing the sick. (vv. 1–2)

Jesus couldn't go anywhere at this point in his ministry without being followed by masses of people, and this was no exception. This is how Jesus finds himself and his disciples looking out over a vast number of people, and he turns to one of his disciples, Philip in this case, and asks what they should do about food. How could they feed all of these people?

It seems his disciples are stumped—all except Andrew, who points out that they do actually have *some* food, but only five loaves of bread and two small fish. How could this possibly help them feed the crowd?

> Jesus said, "Have the people sit down." There was plenty of grass in that place, and they sat down (about five thousand men were there). Jesus then took the loaves, gave thanks, and distributed to those who were seated as much as they wanted. He did the same with the fish.

When they had all had enough to eat, he said to his disciples, "Gather the pieces that are left over. Let nothing be wasted." So they gathered them and filled twelve baskets with the pieces of the five barley loaves left over by those who had eaten. (vv. 10–13)

There is so much going on in this story. Jesus tests his disciples, something that's worthy of an entire chapter of its own. There is Philip giving the factual answer to Jesus' question of where they could get enough food for everyone, and Andrew piping up with the facts of what they had in hand. There is Jesus distributing the food to the crowd, "as much as they wanted."

But there are two small sections I want to emphasize, and the first comes in a verse at the beginning of the passage:

. . . a great crowd of people followed him because they saw the signs he had performed by healing the sick. (v. 2)

Did you catch that? Why was this great crowd of people following Jesus?

Because he had healed their sick. Because his ministry was fruitful.

Here's the second small portion of this passage:

After the people saw the sign Jesus performed, they began to say, "Surely this is the Prophet who is to come into the world." Jesus, knowing that they intended to come and make him king by force, withdrew again to a mountain by himself. (vv. 14–15)

Do you see what's happening here? Jesus provided for the people's needs in a radical way, feeding a huge crowd of them with only the contents of a little boy's lunchbox; and because of this, they see who he really is. Not only this, but they are prepared to make him king on the spot, no matter the consequences. Their motives may have been mixed and their theology scrambled, but this impacted their willingness to hear more and follow the Messiah.

A fruitful church leads to curiosity which leads to Christ followers.

Another way of looking at this comes to us in Romans 2:4: "Or do you show contempt for the riches of his kindness, forbearance and patience, not realizing that God's kindness is intended to lead you to repentance?"

What is intended to lead us to repentance?

God's kindness.

Maybe the fruitful actions, the tangible kindness of the body of Christ, the church, will lead people to repent?

The Byproducts of a Fruitful Church

I had a few questions for my friend Kevin about what happened in his city after the churches dedicated themselves to the peace and prosperity of Portland. What were some of the byproducts of these service-oriented efforts that lead to fruitfulness? Besides the people in the community who were being directly helped, how was the work of the broader, united church changing the people of Portland?

Loving one another. One of my favorite verses in John is 13:35:

> "By this everyone will know that you are my disciples,
> if you love one another."

When Christians and churches turn their focus toward being more fruitful, the community sees this and becomes intrigued. What's going on over there? What are those Christians up to? Why are they helping people they don't even know?

Given the post-everything era, especially with how politicized everyone and everything has become, the divisions between us are seen as massive weaknesses. But when we roll up our sleeves to serve those in need, whether it's refugee support, foster care, or helping our schools, people notice.

Fruitful people love one another, and this changes the way the community views Christians.

It gets the attention of local leaders. Imagine working for your local government, seeing all of the problems and challenges in your community, and then going out to your car and finding an invitation to an Easter service under your windshield wiper? Now, I'm not bashing Easter invitations at all, but in a world that is confronting evil at every turn, I think people, and especially local leaders, are yearning for Christians to help in a practical way—not just offering church services.

So, when compassionate Christians and a united church present themselves to local civic leaders and ask, "How can we help?" this makes sense to those in charge as well as those in the community. Local leaders are almost always compelled by groups who want to help, no matter who they are. Fulfilling the practical needs of community leaders or nonprofit organizations (being fruitful) gets people's attention and opens doors in the future.

The lay person realizes they're not alone. When we as a church become more fruitful, when we show that we can make a difference within this larger framework of service, it gives everyday believers and their pastors a greater confidence in each other and the gospel. This creates a kind of escalating confidence, and everyone begins to feel their strength and courage building. It also provides outlets of service for everyone. The environment of the overall culture might be hostile to the church or the message of the gospel, but moving in fruitful service together allows a certain humility that is also good for the gospel.

We are making a difference!

We have a role in the city!

We're acting as the tangible body of Christ to our neighbors!

These are the kind of sentiments believers start to express when they are working within a fruitful movement, and they develop a kind of boldness that allows for even more good works—it's not an obnoxious boldness, but the kind that allows them to enter into this never-ending battle against injustice, hate, and poverty. And it's this building of boldness that also allows for the gospel to be shared more widely.

Fruitfulness leads to more confident, compassionate Christians.

Builds trust. As the churches and individual Christians begin to see how fruitful the work is, trust is built, not only between the church and the community but even between different denominations. Between various congregations. Between individual believers. Between Christians and their community leaders.

Fruitful results in a community lead to greater trust, which leads to even more fruitful works and increased curiosity in the community around us. There is a debate among some Christians setting up a dichotomy of "social justice" versus "just preach the gospel." Should we do good and right in our community as an avenue for evangelism, or should our focus be solely on preaching the gospel? My view is this: not only are fruitful social justice activities an important reflection of God's heart and the gospel, but our world will increasingly no longer listen to us preaching the gospel unless they see the fruitful social justice work connected to the gospel. A pastor friend of mine in Iowa, Quintin Stieff, says it in a much more memorable way: *Do good works to build good will and you can share the good news.*

Do you see the wonderful side effects that come when we as the church begin to seek out fruitful ways we can serve our communities? Can you understand why this important work needs to come alongside the facts and the truth that we're proclaiming? Fruitful, not just factual.

The Results of Fruitful Living

Remember Roosevelt High School, where the Palau Association and South Lake Church stepped in, hoping to turn a failing school into a better place for its students? Well, for about eight years there was a beautiful partnership between the school and the church. They served the students effectively. Even Nike got involved, rebuilding the track, the grandstand, and the football field. Eventually, Roosevelt received a $20 million makeover. A failing school was saved, catalyzed by the tangible work of a church, whose reputation slowly began to change in the community.

Why the change of perspective?

Because those outside the church saw the fruit, and it was good.

All the church had done was simply to approach their community and city leaders and ask how they could help, how they could serve. Part of it was simply telling a better story about the church, a more accurate story about what many of the churches in the community were already doing. Part of it was providing an opportunity for churches to work together, to pull in churches that had the desire to serve but weren't sure where to begin. Part of it was the intentional effort from those inside the church to live out the fruit of the Spirit within the community.

All of this led to deep and strong relationships with all kinds of people who previously had been antagonistic toward the Portland churches, including Mayor Adams.

Recently, the local churches together with the Palau Association have been asked by the state to become more involved in the foster care program. They started something called Every Child which directly supports 5,000 children entering foster care, giving foster parents much-needed nights out, and church members have even increased their own involvement, becoming foster parents in droves.

The church's work in Portland hasn't stopped there. They've gotten involved in prisoner reentry into the city, refugee care, and a host of other social outreaches. This led to the formation of "The Collective," a collective of Portland area churches and community partners who are heavily involved in serving the needs of the community.

They are showing the world that the gospel is not only factual—it is also fruitful.

Kevin, the Palau organization, and their partner churches are ten years into their work in Portland. They're beginning to realize it's time to take it a step further: While they have been putting an intense amount of effort into being fruitful, into loving and serving the community and rebuilding the church's credibility, they admittedly have taken their eye off the ball when it comes to evangelism. The pendulum swung toward fruitfulness, as it needed to, but Kevin has been sensing the need to increase their evangelism efforts now that a good foundation has been laid.

Fruitfulness and facts can go hand-in-hand. Good works and truth must emerge together.

They've formed an evangelism team, partnering up with Alpha and others, and while the community service continues unabated, they now meet with large Christian groups and senior pastors on a quarterly basis to inspire and equip local believers when it comes to evangelism. The tide is turning.

They want to double the number of churches running the Alpha program.

They want to do occasional large outreaches.

They want to bring in speakers to teach on evangelism.

Evangelism is challenging, and the Palau organization is recommitted to helping local churches become more evangelistically minded, with a goal to help 100 different cities develop an evangelism team that will convene the evangelistically minded leaders in their town and encourage them to dream big.

But I don't think any of these evangelism efforts would work if not for the long, heavy work of fruitfulness in their community—the partnering with schools, the meetings with the mayor, the stepping up and contributing to the foster care system, and so much more.

These are the fruitful works that prepare cities for a fruitful harvest. In order to be fruitful, we can't just go it alone. Let's now discuss how to create an evangelism movement that mobilizes more than just me.

What Next?

- Which of your efforts in the past have been the most fruitful?
- What new ideas do you have to become fruitful in your community?
- Is there a way you can combine fruitful and factual in a compelling way?

6

We, Not Just Me

I showed up for the beginning of a brand-new round of Alpha at our church. The excitement and nervousness in the room was palpable. I love those first few weeks, seeing how interested people are to embark on this new spiritual journey. A collective exhale settles in when guests realize their views won't be judged or criticized. They can bring their whole selves into the conversation—worldviews, wounds, and all.

At this particular Alpha course, one woman stood out. She shared her story with us. She had endured an incredibly difficult past. I'll never forget one of the first things she said.

"My name is April, and I don't believe there's an 'eff-ing' God." Again, no abbreviation.

I honestly don't mind when guests swear at an Alpha group—it's just a reflection of where they are in life, or how they were brought up, or what they're used to. But I could sense some of the people in the group wince. After all, everyone knows you're not supposed to swear in church, right!

April wasn't finished.

"But if there is a God," she continued, "that God had better be prepared to answer why my life has been so screwed up."

Let me be clear—April was not messing around. She didn't say this in a sarcastic manner or leave any of us wondering how serious she was. She was dead serious. Her entire countenance was hostile and hurt. She had such clear wounds from her past, the kind that had seeped into her present and threatened to destroy her life.

This will be interesting, I thought to myself. *And I'm so glad she's here.* I have seen some incredible transformations take place in Alpha courses, but I also knew people like April sometimes stopped coming and we'd never hear from them again. Thankfully, she kept coming.

During the next few weeks, it seemed her sole purpose at Alpha was to dismantle every element of Christianity that was introduced. She chafed at every mention of God and she argued with every statement of faith. I'm not sure I have encountered anyone more hostile than April was during these groups. But we listened. We didn't correct. We didn't redirect. We let her process, just as we allow all guests to react and process.

It was at about that time I had shoulder surgery and missed two weeks of that particular Alpha course. I thought of and prayed for the group often, especially this young woman who was in so much pain. I wondered if she would still be there when I returned, if she would still be angry at God and arguing with everyone.

I recovered and returned to Alpha one night after my short time away. When I first saw April, I was shocked. She was glowing.

Every opportunity that night, during any gap where people could speak, she was passionately trying to convince the atheists in the group that Jesus had changed her life and they needed to know him and fall passionately in love with him!

"He can free you!" she insisted. "God loves you. He wants good things for you. Jesus is real! I'm his and you can be too!"

"Wait a minute," I jumped into the conversation. "What is going on, April?"

I was only gone for two weeks! What could have possibly happened that took April from a place of deep pain and hostility into this new place of transformation, peace, and love?

What's Your Strategy?

When I was a pastor, there were a few questions about our church I heard on repeat, and most of them had to do with strategy. Sometimes other pastors asked me these questions when they were trying to figure out what to do in their own churches. Often, these questions came from new church attendees trying to figure out how to navigate our community.

What's your youth ministry strategy?
What's your connections strategy?
What's your groups strategy?
What's your volunteer mobilization strategy?
What's your parking lot strategy?
What's your coffee bar strategy?

You get the idea. When you're a pastor, you tend to be the point person for a lot of different "strategies." But one of the questions I admittedly had difficulty answering was:

What's your evangelism strategy?

Some pastors have programs in place aimed at spreading the gospel or helping their congregations spread the gospel in their communities. Other pastors might not be able to verbalize what their strategy is. Evangelism efforts, and how to create a strategy around them, can often feel hard to pin down.

My real (somewhat embarrassing and sometimes unspoken) answer to that question was, "It's me, the pastor. I'm the primary evangelism strategy of the church." Ugh. No matter the programs, no matter the strategies, the truth is this: The number one evangelism strategy in the majority of western churches is the pastor. Pastors are called, equipped, and gifted, and the unwritten contract between pastor and congregation is often, "You get them into church, and I'll seal the deal." The agreement is that if you invite your friends and get them through the front doors of the church on a Sunday morning, the pastor will create an experience and deliver a message that brings them back, over and over, until they make a commitment to follow Christ.

And this works. Every single weekend, churches all around the world are leading people to faith in Christ with hand-raising moments and response times. I support altar calls and pastors sharing the good news every week. This kind of me-based evangelism is extremely important, and pastors should continue being a primary or significant evangelism strategy at their church.

I am not here to dismantle the power of me-based pastor evangelism.

But the meta-data is telling us that me-based strategies are not enough on their own.

Not everyone in our community is showing up for these moments. Not everyone is waking up on a Sunday morning and deciding to go through the front door or click through the online service portal of a church. Not everyone is willing, or interested in, sitting down and listening to someone else talk at them about Jesus. Church attendance in every generation is in decline, so we cannot depend only on me-based pastor evangelism, the kind of model where one person is designated as the sharer to the masses in church services.

Depending on lots of factors, it's still somewhat effective, but not nearly effective enough.

Many churches have a secondary evangelism strategy, and it's also a me-based strategy. We train individuals for personal evangelism. In other words, we attempt to give people the tools they need to go out into the world and share their faith with someone else. We mostly conduct this training through weekend services and messages, but there are also a great many training curricula and classes that help pastors and leaders equip their congregations.

And I love them.

There are many solid programs out there that will help you do this well.

I think we should still be doing this.

But what I found when I was a pastor, after leading thousands of people in my own church through some of these top-rate programs, was that they primarily only maximized people with the gift of evangelism. Those extroverts with the gift of evangelism were on fire and bearing fruit, and the tools we gave them through these me-based training programs took them to another level.

But those without the gift of evangelism? Those who weren't experts or extroverts or people already leaning toward sharing their faith one-on-one with their neighbors and friends? They were still in the same place, struggling with the concept of evangelism, except now they were weighed down with guilt for their lack of performance.

I remember at one point, looking at the fruitfulness (or lack of it) in my own church. I considered all the resources and effort we were putting into these evangelism training programs. I thought about how I was working harder than ever on my sermons. I reflected on how intensely I was working to equip individuals to share their faith. I had to admit none of it was dramatically moving the needle leading many to a new relationship in Jesus Christ. Some of it worked and some said "yes," but the numbers of people finding Christ in our church community wasn't increasing exponentially. I was praying for and working for a tidal wave, but only seeing what amounted to a trickle compared to the hundreds of thousands of people in our region who didn't know the love of Christ.

I started digging into this issue. We asked the people in our large, evangelism-focused church to take spiritual gift assessments, and what we discovered was rather eye-opening: Only 4 percent of church attendees actually had the gift of evangelism in their top three spiritual gifts. Only 4 percent! The Barna Group reports the number has declined in the broader US from 4 percent in the mid 1990s to 1 percent now.[1] No wonder evangelism is so difficult! No wonder it's so hard for pastors and congregations to turn the needle and mobilize the masses when our primary strategies aren't working with the strengths of 96 percent or more of our people.

But those people are still called to fulfill the Great Commission, right? All of us are called to "Go and make disciples of all nations." Just like we are all called to pray, although not all of us have the gift of intercessory prayer.

Those who have the gift of evangelism will take what they need from sermons and training programs, and they'll get out there and do their thing. But what about the rest?

How are we equipping those saints to share their faith in ways that are not me-based? How can you personally grow at sharing your faith more effectively whether you have the gift of evangelism or not? Maybe there is another way, but before we get there, a few more observations.

There's another disadvantage of me-based evangelism,

and that's how it unintentionally hides the spiritual journey and discovery behind individualistic moments. What happens when someone in a one-on-one relationship receives the gift of Christ? In a me-based evangelism situation, too often the only person who is connected with this new believer, the only person present during that wonderful moment of decision, is that one Christian who led them down the path. This sort of isolated conversion means other non-Christians miss the best miracle possible: watching people who feel far from God discover life in Christ.

The me-based evangelistic model all but removes others (both Christians and non-Christians) from this new believer's introduction to faith, their journey to faith, and their decision to follow Christ. Too few Christians are able to travel along the journey of discipleship that a person takes from being a non-Christian to becoming a sustaining faith-filled believer in Christ. And too few non-Christians are impacted by seeing that life-changing conversion before their very eyes.

If our me-based evangelism strategies are not deliberately connected to a group experience or community, we can see a trend where possibly hundreds of thousands of people respond in a moment, yet their faith often fizzles without a quick insertion into a life and community of discipleship. Where are they the following week or where is their transformed life the following year? And, their witness is hampered because the spiritual journey often happened anonymously or in private. Maybe you've seen it yourself: hundreds or even thousands of hands raised or steps walked to the front of the church or digital response forms submitted—but where are they now?

With Whom Are You Eating?

Jesus shows us a different way: a shift to we, not just me.

We see this we-based, broad-reaching evangelism strategy in Jesus' ministry from the very beginning, even in the way he called his very first disciples. He regularly placed himself in groups where he was surrounded by outsiders, interacting graciously with groups of people outside the religious crowd, and this approach became a powerful tool for bringing people into the kingdom.

Jesus' strategy pulled together the explicitly untrained, yet freshly passionate Levi (Matthew) with a group of his very messy non-Jesus-following friends and acquaintances. Try to imagine some of the conversations around that table full of tax collectors.

"Yo, you should have seen the look on that guy's face when I told him everything in his wallet was mine. I just smirked, took another swig of that Jerusalem wine, you know the stuff that costs a month's wages, and laughed him out of the room!"

"You guys should have been at that party on the west side the other day, I can't even describe how wild it got."

You get the picture. I'm guessing they weren't exactly refined. Yet Jesus knew this was the perfect setting for people to find faith—in a group. An extremely messy group.

The religious authorities considered eating with tax

collectors as completely out of bounds, and yet Jesus associated with Levi, and Levi decided to follow him and gathered the group.

The image of Jesus witnessing to Levi might seem a nice example of me-based evangelism. But this is where me-based evangelism often, sadly, ends. The convert has been saved. They have made a decision for Christ. Too many churches, too many Christians, move on, looking for the next convert.

But Jesus' commitment to we-based evangelism meant that when Levi held a great banquet in his honor, Jesus didn't hesitate to attend, even though they were joined by "a large crowd of tax collectors and others."

Note what Jesus didn't do.

He didn't discourage Levi from inviting his tax collector friends to this gathering. Jesus didn't tell Levi, "You're a new creation now—no more spending time with that riff-raff." It seems clear by what Jesus later told the Pharisees that he recognized this opportunity to spend time with the "sick" of society as a chance to invite them to journey with him.

Something else that Jesus didn't do was avoid this gathering in favor of getting each tax collector into a one-on-one situation or to a service at the temple or even into a group of confirmed disciples; instead, he pulled the non-disciples together. In other words, Jesus didn't shy away from gatherings where he was outnumbered by spiritually lost people. He seemed to seek out these places throughout the life of his ministry.

Third, Jesus didn't hide or keep secret these times he spent with tax collectors and sinners. It wasn't something he was ashamed of or something he did in the dead of night. Throughout the Gospels, Jesus made time for "sinners"—it's clear he did it often, and he did it in the open. I have to wonder the effect that this mindset had on the marginalized and outcast—"This popular rabbi, this amazing teacher, this miracle worker, spends time with us, and he's not ashamed of it! Even when the religious leaders confront him about it, he doesn't back down!"

Is that something the marginalized in our communities or those outside the church can say about us and the people in our churches? Do non-Christians regularly marvel that we're willing to spend time with them? Are we known as friends—like Jesus?

And, have we created spaces within our church evangelism strategies and personal lives for gathering outsiders? Or is it primarily a me-based, Sunday morning, personal evangelism training and Christian-small-group-only model reinforcing the us-versus-them mentality so prevalent in our society today? Do we live individually entering spaces of outsiders and creating places at our tables for groups of those outside the faith?

Do our tables look like the tables where Jesus sat?

Jesus often evangelized by bringing groups of "unbelieving outsiders" together, allowing them to eat and drink and talk about life and even faith and following God. Jesus often did more ministry around tables than he did within the temple. And that's my suggestion, one of the forgotten

141

ways of effective evangelism is the power of groups exploring together, in conversation, around a table. (And with
great food and drink, of course!)

Maybe you're listening to all of this and thinking,
*You've got to be kidding me, Craig. There is no way I'm going to
get a bunch of rough-edged atheists or those hostile toward faith
together and have them dismantle the authority of Scripture
and the supernatural reality of the resurrection, all within
earshot of each other. All they are going to do is compound
their own doubts. And especially now, as I'm beginning to
discover you want me to primarily listen and draw out their
questions!*

There is no way this is going to work.

And yet, by every experience and metric we have seen,
it does work. It also worked for Jesus, who gathered outsiders in groups and asked almost 40 times more questions
than he provided direct answers.

First, as we talked about earlier in the book, the sense
of belonging which arises from these groups has transformative power. People are learning what it means to start out
on a spiritual journey of faith in community. That power of
belonging lowers walls and opens hearts and minds through
the power of listening and discussion. People begin their
journey seeing what it's like to be part of a beautiful community that takes on kingdom values. This sets them up for
a spiritual life of staying connected to community rather
than seeking out individualistic moments.

Second, the curiosity of faith has a startling, positive
domino effect. It is disarming to see other people carry

doubt, not be judged, and then make progress over time. People start to see others come to faith, they start to see these new friends experience breakthroughs in relationships and forgiveness and healing, and they start to want in too. Their excitement begins to gather momentum and rub off on each other, and they begin to open their eyes, discovering Christ together. Agnostic and atheist guests alike see converts to Christ and say, "Wow! What has happened to you? Last week you were one person, but this week you're totally changed! Now I'm more open than ever."

This is the power of inclusive, we-based evangelism. It makes sense because of Romans 1:16: "For I am not ashamed of the gospel, because it is the power of God that brings salvation to everyone who believes." When we don't hide the gospel journey in me-based moments, its power spreads to others around the table. It's what Jesus knew was at work at Levi's table.

What's in It for Me?

Here's another surprising benefit of we-based evangelism. Often when we discuss evangelism efforts, our main concern is the convert. In other words, we try to consider what is most effective in saving a lost person without taking into account how it is impacting the Christians we are equipping.

Ger Jones, a fantastic pastor in Los Angeles, identifies ways that this small-group, we-based evangelism continues to benefit the Christians who volunteer as hosts in these settings. Ger has structured evangelism strategy around Alpha for many years and has developed some helpful reflections from each iteration.

It equips everyone. We-based evangelism, and specifically for Ger the Alpha program, gathers people into groups for faith exploration and equips everyone with an easy and effective evangelistic tool that they can participate in. It's something Christians can easily do to help their friends start on a spiritual journey toward Christ.

A large number of people who attend church theoretically want to do evangelism, but they feel it's practically beyond them, or they don't feel equipped, or they feel older methods are impossible or too confrontational. They worry that if their non-Christian friends ask questions, they won't know the answers. Or maybe they feel like their own faith isn't strong enough. They worry about being socially rejected or that if they bring their friends to church, it ends up being an embarrassing experience. One friend of mine, recalling the moment he was invited to a Christian gathering for the first time said, "You get one shot. If I go and hate it or feel judged, that's it; you can never ever talk to me about this again." That's a lot of pressure!

Anyone who has shared their faith knows the feeling that comes the next time you see that friend. You wonder if they think you're crazy or if the friendship is now somehow compromised. In most cases, we haven't given church members in this post-Christian era an evangelism methodology that feels helpful or effective.

But when people participate in small-group evangelism efforts such as Alpha, they see their non-Christian friends actually enjoying themselves! What a game-changer, to have a tool for evangelism where the person being told about Christianity actually enjoys the process! So many other evangelism efforts become negative experiences for both the Christian and the person they're trying to share with. But small-group based evangelism (grounded with listening and belonging) gives everyone a tool and experience that is helpful.

The invite can become as simple as inviting someone to enjoy a great meal and then to watch a documentary on faith with the space to share their thoughts and opinions without correction. When Christians begin to see both how easy and how effective this type of evangelism can be, they are motivated to change how they live, building more friendships outside of the church. They know they have an effective and easy invitation and want to fill the seats the next time the table gathers with those outside the church. This is how we can mobilize the entire congregation to get active and invitational. We've created a new front door for their friends and a table they want to be at, together.

No evangelism experts required. In most churches, we've delegated evangelism to the experts: pastors, authors, and conference speakers, or those bold, select, and gifted few in the congregation. But in most cases, this is quite limited because many people aren't initially all that interested in going to church on a Sunday morning and being preached to, and they're hesitant about engaging in a religious debate.

If we're not delegating our evangelism to the experts, then we're probably delegating it to the extroverts. There is a small percentage of people in every congregation who don't care what people think of them, and those people are willing to preach the gospel to any random person who stops long enough to talk to them.

But most of us aren't like that. Most of us don't have that gift.

We-based evangelism takes evangelism and makes it accessible to those of us who aren't experts or extroverts. Jesus calls everyone to be witnesses of who he was—Alpha, as an example of this, helps every Christian fulfill this mission. It mobilizes the entire church and opens up entire networks of people to hear the gospel.

A deep love and empathy. Participating in this kind of small-group-based evangelism, centered around listening, gives the Christians in the group a deep love and empathy for non-Christians. Typical Christendom can often create an us versus them mentality—who's right, who's wrong, who's in, who's out.

But in contexts like Alpha, through listening and time, genuine friendships emerge among participants and Christian hosts or helpers form deep empathy for everyone else in the group; what they've been through, and why they are where they are on their spiritual journey. They are no longer targets but people loved by God who have been shaped by pain, confusing circumstances, or disconnected relationships along the way.

Everyone has a story behind their world view. No one

comes to a position of spirituality out of a neutral journey. We all have experiences and relationships that have shaped our beliefs, yet many Christians don't often create enough space and time to acknowledge this, not in themselves and not in others. When we are able to see the story, we love people differently, we listen more intently, we help more wholeheartedly.

Contexts such as Alpha cultivate in the Christian a love for the lost, helping them transition from being primarily frustrated with the lost. It's a love that can unlock someone's heart to the gospel.

The ripple effect. People who participate in a small-group evangelism experience take what they learn about listening and creating spaces of belonging and weave that into the larger body and life of their church. Everyone who does Alpha becomes a better leader in the areas where they contribute, from the nursery to the worship band, from greeting to teaching. They become more empathetic, better listeners, and they don't preach to people as much.

They basically become better hosts.

The conversion effect. There are two different types of non-Christians today, each of which are responsive in varied way. The types are the lapsed and the lost. The lapsed are those who grew up in church, have a relatively accessible gospel heritage or memory, and have walked away. The lost are those who may have never even heard the gospel.

It is a beautiful thing, when the lapsed raise their hands in church and recommit their lives to Christ. Also, small-group-based evangelism can be a wonderful tool to help that happen.

But what Christians in the West aren't seeing as much these days are lost people finding Christ who have absolutely no background connected to church or the Christian faith. Many Christians look at Buddhists, atheists, or others who have never gone to church and think, *They're a lost cause.* Maybe they don't say that out loud, but practically speaking, it's what they've accepted. Spaces of conversation and listening within a group are often the best first front door for the lost to begin engaging with the gospel, rather than a church service designed for the already convinced or more effective at reaching the lapsed. We see many more lost people coming to faith in Christ through efforts such as Alpha, who then find their way into the greater body of Christ and other church activities after that initial group experience.

How could that person ever find Christ?

When people see a lost person discover Christ, it changes everything. It raises their faith. They realize God *can* break through, even in this post-Christian culture. They realize, because they see it firsthand, we don't have to be concerned and fearful that we are going to be overwhelmed by our culture. The power of the gospel has always been and will always be more powerful than a cultural movement.

Seeing a new conversion is so faith-affirming. People's hope for their friends is restored. Every conversion is a miracle. It's exciting to see Christians rediscover the power of the gospel and believe that anyone can be saved—and it can start with a simple, enjoyable invitation.

Seeing the gospel at work. Alpha is exciting for Christians because much of today's American Christianity functions as something we hold to intellectually. And while Alpha teaches the intellectual doctrines of the faith, it also showcases them, demonstrating them. Alpha creates space for the Holy Spirit to move in people's lives in real ways through prayer for healing, inviting people to receive the love of the Father, and through people praying to receive salvation in Christ. These are some of what we discussed in the chapter on experience, not just explanation.

Ger says that the gospel always comes in three ways: words, works, and wonders. Words of the gospel, works of love, and wonders of the Spirit. So many Christians only ever experience the words. They're told to do the works. They've certainly never encountered the wonders.

Alpha provides an environment for all three. That was the ministry of Jesus and is to be the ministry of the church. Alpha creates an environment where all three happen at the same time.

Exponential growth. Finally, when you put Christians into a group with non-Christians, the Christians will grow exponentially in their own faith because they suddenly must wrestle with the questions that most non-Christians are wrestling with. Wading through these issues causes the Christian volunteer to grow stronger.

They also have to help disciple new believers—not just listen, but really get involved in the life of a new believer. Most Christians today see themselves as the recipient of discipleship—in other words, most Christians believe they are being discipled but do not consider themselves capable of discipling others. But Alpha and other small group-based evangelism efforts set up the entire church to be disciplers.

The we-based evangelism that takes place in contexts like Alpha begins to develop confidence and growth in the everyday Christian and opens up a brand-new front door into the church that the non-Christian hasn't had before. Most of us have a difficult time transitioning the conversations with our neighbors from how the Broncos played last night to an exegetical analysis of substitutionary atonement theory. Taking that leap in a conversation can be difficult for someone who's not gifted in evangelism—that's 96 percent of Christians, remember? So, we create a space at a dinner where someone will be listened to, and belong, and experience the power of a community interested in Christ.

But what does the data say?

It's compelling.

Eighty-two percent of non-Christians who complete an Alpha course—a small-group based, listening-centered process—develop a relationship with Jesus by the time the course is completed (2016 Barna impact study of Alpha participants).

Seventy-eight percent of lapsed Christians, those who may have attended church as children but are no longer involved in a meaningful way, report dramatically increasing their involvement in their local church community after going through Alpha (2016 Barna impact study of Alpha participants).

That is potent.

That is the we, not just me, evangelism of Jesus.

What Happened to April?

So, what became of April, the woman at the beginning of the chapter who was so full of anger and pain and then one week showed up at Alpha proclaiming God's goodness?

What did she experience that so profoundly changed her view of Jesus?

She said, "I went home after one of the weeks at Alpha and I felt an overwhelming urge to fall to my knees. I just started crying, and I couldn't stop. I didn't understand what was happening, and I just started calling out to God, shouting and crying, and that's when I heard something like a spiritual voice speaking to me."

"I love you, April. You are my beloved."

"I just knew it was God," she told our Alpha group, with tears in her eyes. "I knew it. And I felt a blanket of warmth wrap around me, and I sensed the voice of Christ. I poured out my heart, my need for him, and I said I was his. I felt a healing presence over the hurts I'd been carrying."

She paused, and everyone else (who had already heard this story by now because I was just back from back surgery) listened and leaned in again.

"I gave my life to Jesus."

This is what can happen when we engage in we-based evangelism.

But it didn't stop there. By the end of that group, three

of the other people who said they were atheists and agnostics gave their lives to Christ as well.

Why?

What in the world was it about April's experience of Jesus finding her that spoke to the rest of the group?

That's an easy one to answer. They had experienced the greatest miracle of all: an actual conversion of someone from spiritual death to life, someone whom they had known, whom they had walked with, someone they had even passionately shared a worldview with. They had seen her anger and her unbelief. Yet, they also saw her authentic journey toward Christ right in front of their eyes happen over a few weeks' time.

And she had become a follower of Jesus at their table.

They were able to be part of her community, learn alongside her, and when she encountered Christ, I know at least a few of them thought, "Well, if that happened to April, then God *must* be real." And they said "yes" to Jesus too. I have to imagine that's also what happened at Levi's tax collector party.

This is the beautiful thing about we-based evangelism.

What if we in the church created a group experience based on all the elements we've talked about?

Many people today aren't initially interested in coming to church or impacted by what they experience if they do, but what if evangelism is as simple as inviting someone to dinner?

What if it's as simple as promising a table where they'll be listened to, not judged, and experience the kind of community they probably haven't experienced before?

We, not just me. The way of Jesus. In this our communities will be positioned for the most powerful posture they can possibly achieve, which we will explore next.

What Next?

- How could your evangelism strategy become more "we" based?
- Which of the benefits of small-group based evangelism as described by Ger Jones strikes you as the most beneficial for your specific community?
- If April came to your church, in her original state, would your church have a place for her to grow and process over time?

7

Unity, Not Just Uniformity

On January 6, 2017, a man opened fire on a crowd of people near the baggage claim in Terminal 2 of the Fort Lauderdale International Airport. The shooting itself lasted fewer than two minutes, at which point the shooter laid down on the ground, having run out of ammunition. He was apprehended by law enforcement officials—no further shots were fired.

Later the horrifying numbers came in: Five people had been killed and six injured by the shooting, and a further thirty-six were hurt in the ensuing panic. Forty-seven lives changed.

It was the early days of Church United, an organization seeking to bring unity to churches in south Florida, and Eddie Copeland, the leader of the organization, was staring at his computer reading the headlines mentioned above.

Through prayers and heartache, Eddie had an idea. Church United was still a new organization, and he had been working hard to get these churches to cooperate, but he sensed a new way that they could come together and serve their community in the wake of this tragedy . . . if all the churches were willing. He sent out an email to the lead team, asking, "What if we went to the city and said we'd pay for all the medical bills of the people injured by the shooting? Could we do this? How much do we think we could raise?"

He asked around and got a ballpark figure of what that number might be.

In 24 hours, the united churches of Broward County had come together to raise double what they needed in order to pay the medical bills of all 47 people who were treated.

Now, all he had to do was talk to those in charge of the city so that he could deliver the funds. He called the mayor of Fort Lauderdale, and once he was able to get through to him, he delivered a very simple message.

"Hi, my name is Eddie Copeland, and I represent Church United, a consortium of churches in south Florida. We would like to pay all the medical bills of those injured in the shooting."

At first, silence. And then, "Wait a minute. What church are you from?"

Eddie was taken aback. He had a big check for them, but the person seemed at least a little bit disgruntled, or at least uncertain. Who was Eddie, and what was the spin on this offer? There had to be some kind of spin on it. No one would just call in randomly and offer to pay thousands and thousands of dollars of medical bills for strangers.

"I said, I'm calling on behalf of the churches in south Florida."

"Are you saying all the churches have come together and want to pay the medical bills?"

"Yes, that's what I'm saying."

Silence.

"Okay, hold on a minute."

Eventually, after a few different conversations and a few days later, Eddie walked into Broward General Hospital, where those affected were being treated. He delivered the rather large check to the general manager of the hospital, who was not a Christian, and at first the man just held the check in his hand and stared at it. Then he looked up at Eddie.

"Walk me through this again. Which churches did this?"

Eddie gave him a list of the churches which had donated toward the effort. The man wrinkled his brow.

"What exactly is it you all want?"

"I'm sorry?" Eddie asked.

"What do you want?" the man asked again. "Is this a media story? Are you trying to get some PR? What do you all want in exchange for this?"

Eddie smiled and shook his head. "I haven't contacted anyone in the media. We just love this city and feel like there's something we can do to help alleviate the pain and suffering of those who were injured."

The man still seemed to think it was too good to be true, but he took a deep breath.

"Would you write me a paragraph, basically what you just said, so that I can send it to the 47 patients whose bills you all are paying?"

"Of course!" Eddie said, and he did. Eventually, the hospital sent out that letter to those 47 patients, and it said, "Your bills have been paid for by the churches of Broward County, in Jesus' name." Wow.

Church United did ultimately get the city's attention, though they didn't seek it out. And when Hurricane Irma swept in, with storm surges flooding highways and high winds eliminating power from six million households, they were there for the community again. Church United became the backbone facilitator for the broader church and led much of the relief effort in that area. All the churches involved were beginning to see what it looked like to have a unified response—they were working together with congregations they had never even spoken with before. They were meeting each other and realizing the Christians at other churches, with whom they had some doctrinal disagreements, weren't terrible people.

They could impact their community together.

But the airport shooting and the hurricane were only the beginning.

What's Keeping People Away

Think about this example for a moment.

Imagine you're back in middle school again (I know, sorry to introduce a negative limbic reaction for you). You get home from school, maybe hang out in your room for a bit, and you figure it's going to be dinner time soon so you head to the kitchen, only to hear your parents having a very loud argument. Their voices are mean and angry, and their words are cutting. You pause, sort of shrink into yourself a little bit, and quietly retreat to your bedroom.

There's no way you're getting into the middle of that.

Now imagine you're an innocent bystander in today's society. You have questions about spirituality and God; you wonder about the nature of the universe. You are hoping for deeper significance in life. You find yourself thinking philosophical thoughts every once in a while, and you'd love a place to go and explore these ideas. Or maybe you've experienced major pain in your life, and you are looking around for a safe place to process it.

You wonder if your local church might be a good environment to track down some answers, but then you watch the news or glance through social media and you see churches, as well as untold Christians, at complete odds with one another. You see Christian leaders arguing with other Christian leaders. You see division after division of what seems like angry Christian chaos; followers of Jesus who can't get along with each other.

There's no way you're getting into the middle of that.

Spiritually curious non-Christians reported in *Reviving Evangelism* that one of *the* primary factors which would cause them to be more open to faith "is if I saw more churches working together."[1] Is that a surprising insight for you? Honestly, I wasn't expecting that to show up in the data, but it makes sense now that I see it.

Our disunity is keeping people from the church, keeping people from a meaningful encounter with a community of Christ followers. Our disunity is keeping people away from Jesus. It's off-putting and uncomfortable, and it makes it easy for an already skeptical public to simply walk away. *Why would I want to follow Christ when Christ followers and Christian churches are constantly arguing and throwing stones at one another?*

An increasingly crucial part of this evolving world of evangelism is building friendships with churches and other Christians we feel far away from. The world just doesn't see this enough—churches spending time together, working together, praying together, having fun together, Christians building bridges across lines of perceived doctrinal and historical division. After all, when was the last time your church reached out to a neighboring congregation? When was the last time your church did a service project with another church, or a prayer night, or teamed up to do vacation Bible school, or anything substantial together? Or when is the last time you connected deeply with a fellow Christian from a different traditional background?

It happens so infrequently.

Let me clarify this right away—when I talk about unity, I'm not talking about uniformity, a kind of assimilation where we all must believe the same things and think the same things and see every aspect of minor theology in the same way. That is a long way from happening and not even necessary. I'm also not talking about dropping the core message of Christ and the awareness of sin; I'm not talking about watering down the gospel. No, I'm talking about gospel-centered, Christian unity that has as its common core the death and resurrection of Jesus Christ; salvation through Christ alone. It carries an agreement that sin is sin and we must be forgiven by Jesus, die to ourselves and walk a new, sanctified path of discipleship in him and his ways. Christian unity majors in the majors but it minors in the minors.

Yet there are many of us out here who share these core beliefs, the majors, but have still been divided for years over so many peripheral things: how to worship, how to do church, what kind of building to do church in, how we feel about Luther, how we feel about liturgy, how we feel about gender roles in church leadership, how we feel about Mary, how we interpret the end times, who can be baptized, what's the best way to participate in communion, and who is allowed to take communion. The list truly goes on and on.

Listen, I have opinions on many of those issues. Some of my opinions are quite strong and, for the most part, are founded on decades of my own Bible study and reading and hearing what other smart theologians have to say about the topics. However, many of the issues and my related opinions could be categorized as "disputable matters," not core tenets of the gospel. If we choose to remain divided over these "disputable matters," and if we continue to isolate ourselves from people who disagree with us in the minors, we'll end up with a billion churches that each have limited impact on the world around us. We'll end up pushing more people away from Jesus.

What if God made some portions of truth crystal clear and left other portions of truth somewhat inconclusive as part of his strategy to remind us we don't and can't know all things and to keep us from acting as if we did? In humility, we must embrace some level of charity to other Christians who see inconclusive issues outside the gospel differently than ourselves.

What if the Lord wants us all to live and reflect as the apostle Paul:

> For I resolved to know nothing while I was with you except Jesus Christ and him crucified.
>
> 1 Corinthians 2:2

Isn't that the core of the core? Go ahead and read that verse one more time. We can remain uniform, like within our families. We can have faith tribes and denominations and collectives with greater common good and shared values around certain matters of theology and practice. But uniformity alone will keep us from unity, where we can resolve to "know nothing except Jesus Christ" together.

Interestingly, the Father, Son, and Holy Spirit—the Trinity—are uniform in their character but not uniform in their function or expression as distinct persons in the godhead. They are always unified though. As we reflect the image of God as the whole Christian church, we can maintain some uniformity within our theological circles, but we have some growing to do to reflect the unity of the Lord across the broader Christian church.

Part of effective evangelism in this day and age means building friendships across the Christian lines that have normally divided us. The real need is for deeper unity when the world is crying out for help and hope.

So the World May Believe

If we want the world to know that Christ is the way, the truth, and the life—then we need to follow *the* recipe Jesus gave us for the world to know.

Consider these words of Jesus in John 17:20–23:

> "My prayer is not for them alone. I pray also for those who will believe in me through their message, that all of them may be one, Father, just as you are in me and I am in you. May they also be in us so that the world may believe that you have sent me. I have given them the glory that you gave me, that they may be one as we are one—I in them and you in me—so that they may be brought to complete unity. Then the world will know that you sent me and have loved them even as you have loved me."

These are some of Jesus' last words to his followers, reinforcing the most important elements he wanted his crew to remember on the very night of his betrayal and arrest.

"That all of them may be one."

"May they also be in us."

"I have given them the glory that you gave me, that they may be one as we are one . . .

. . . so that they may be brought to complete unity . . ."

Again and again in these verses is Jesus' revolutionary prayer and vision for what his followers might be like in the coming time. He reiterates the importance of unity, of remaining as one in the world. But why? Why would Jesus spend these precious remaining moments of his life "nagging" his disciples about the importance of sticking together, of remaining as one, of continuing to be unified?

Part of it, I think, is that he knew what a challenge it would be. He could see the issues on the horizon, things such as whether Gentiles could be saved, whether it was necessary to be circumcised, and what would happen when they began to be seriously persecuted. He could see the fissures that would form, the separations that might occur, the alliances within his own group of disciples that could be formed and fractured.

He saw all of the disunity coming.

But he also recognized that unity would be one of the church's most effective tools of evangelism.

"May they also be in us so that the world may believe.
. . . that they may be brought to complete unity.
Then the world will know that you sent me and have loved them even as you have loved me."

Do you see the direct correlation between unity and belief?

When the world sees a unified church, the gospel message is finally visible and so much more compelling.

Five Important Things About Unity

Dr. Stacy Spencer is the senior pastor of New Direction Christian Church in Memphis, Tennessee. Their congregation meets at several other sites as well, including Collierville, Tennessee, and Idutwya, South Africa. While Dr. Spencer has written multiple books and influenced so much change in the church, one of the things I appreciate most about him is his commitment to church unity.

"You know," he told me recently, "the church is so thoroughly divided around race, particularly in the South, that we've allowed racism to shape our theology. Instead of us being unified on Sunday mornings, it's still one of the most segregated hours in the deep South. Racism and disunity have manifested itself in churches. Many outside the church, unfortunately, have misappropriated that angst, that racism, with our beloved Christian faith, simply because of some who support this vitriol."

"We should be walking together hand in hand."

Recently, Dr. Spencer has started conversations that involve thousands of people, all centered around issues of equity and justice and how they can make Memphis a city for everyone.

"When everyone is sitting together in the same place,"

he said, "working together and establishing God's kingdom on earth as it is in heaven, that's an echo of what the kingdom of God should really look like."

Dr. Stacy Spencer is a fountain of knowledge and grace, and his desire for unity is second to none. Here are five important things about unity that he has taught me:

1. *People aren't always looking for churches—they're looking for friends.* This might be hard for some to hear, especially pastors, but think about why people come to your place of worship on Sunday morning. People don't think they need the organizational or structural component which churches often bring. What they really need is the relational, community aspect of church along with the message of Christ to strengthen their discipleship. And the unity we're talking about begins inside a church, with loving relationships between fellow churchgoers. This love and sense of belonging eventually makes its way out beyond the church into the community as we seek unity with other believers.

Dr. Spencer is part of an organization called Micah: It's "a coalition for action and hope." In Micah, congregations and community organizations come together so that their voices for justice and equity can be amplified. More importantly, Micah fills a void in the community. It's a place where people can become friends with people who aren't like them, and where these people from different backgrounds can work together to impact their community.

2. *We can do more when we stop operating in silos.* As Dr. Martin Luther King Jr. said, "No man is an island," and, "In a real sense all life is inter-related. All men are

caught in an inescapable net of mutuality, tied in a single garment of destiny. Whatever effects one directly effects all indirectly."

There is power in numbers, and if we want to achieve our collective potential, we have to learn how to work together, to unite with our brothers and sisters. Dr. Spencer told me of an African proverb that says, *when spider webs unite, they can tie up a lion.* Together we can tackle racism and economic issues, like systemic poverty and inadequate school resources.

There is power in numbers. A cord of three strands is not easily broken. Where two or three are gathered . . .

3. *Integrating the work of social justice with the work of the gospel is key.* As Dr. Spencer puts it, "We've been conditioned, all the way back since slave times, that we don't need to be worried about earthly conditions because everything will be taken care of 'in the sweet by and by.' That's a slave religion that made people focus on the other-worldly rewards, rather than the equality offered by Jesus in the here-and-now abundant life."

For a long time, some Christians have been concerned by the term "social gospel"—that our concern for alleviating poverty or hunger or homelessness or racism is taking precedence over our concern for spreading the gospel of Jesus. Dr. Spencer rightly contends that unity brings us to realize you cannot separate the work of social justice from the truth of the gospel. They go hand in hand.

4. *People begin to view other people differently when they're invited into unity.* When we start practicing unity,

when we begin to walk in the shoes of our neighbors, we suddenly have empathy for one another. We start to establish relationships with those who are different from us. We start traveling to the other side of town and changing the narrative. We become motivated to stop institutional discrimination and division, and change legislation in a way that benefits our neighbor.

When we listen to the stories of those around us, we realize we have more in common than we do otherwise. How can two agree unless they walk together?

5. *When people experience unity, they become more empowered to share the good news.* There's no question, when Christians experience a greater sense of unity with other Christians from other congregations, they become bolder both in sharing the truth of the gospel in their community and also in starting helpful new initiatives.

Dr. Spencer tells the story of some people who found out about redlining in their community, a discriminatory practice where banks and realtors refuse to loan or give services to people of color in specific communities. Subsequently, they began echoing the stories of other people who had experienced systemic challenges, and they collectively began working with a bank to get large sums of money directed into their communities. They started bringing people from the community to these meetings so that they could buy their own homes. This only happened through a unified effort of carrying the burdens of one another.

There's another story of a business owner who had his own staffing agency, and he started giving a chance to young men being released from prison. They couldn't find work anywhere, so he decided he'd work with them personally. One young man got his CDL through the staffing agency and began driving a truck. Finally, he was able to provide for his family without stealing or selling drugs or committing violent crimes.

When Dr. Spencer met him, he was beaming.

"The small cabin I have to sleep in on the road inside my truck seems like a mansion compared to the cell I had to sleep in for seven years. And now I get to see America, something I couldn't see from my prison bars."

Do you see how the work of unity paves the road to freedom?

Pre-Requisites for Unity

I'm sensitive to how calls for unity can backfire or even become weaponized to perpetuate the pain of many, particularly when it comes to the issues of ethnic unity. With the prevalence of racism and injustices which plague our country and beyond, calls for unity from those with power and privilege can sound tone deaf at best or abusive at worst to others choking under the kneecap of oppression. When some cry out for idealized racial unity, saying things like, "I don't see color," others cry out with realism, saying, "But I can't breathe!" Calls for unity from the "haves" can be encoded attempts or perceived as encoded attempts for the "have-nots" to "stop complaining, stop crying wolf, and get with the program, on my terms." This only keeps the voices of the oppressed silenced while their real needs remain.

For unity to exist we must hear the voices of the oppressed and address their concerns. This will lead to equity.

Unity cannot exist without equity. Equity cannot exist without justice. We will never be able to achieve the unity of Christ and an effective witness to this world without first investing in the building blocks of equity and justice; they are pre-requisites of true unity. It's helpful to consider this concept through the analogy of someone trapped in a physically abusive marriage. An abuser may say to their spouse, "Honey, let's have a great relationship; let's be together," and even apologize for past abuses. Yet the abuses continue, the beatings are covered up, and days later the cries for a healthy, unified marriage continue. To the abused spouse, the concepts of a healthy, unified marriage is manipulative and impossible until the abuses stop and the wrongs are made right.

Many of my friends who are people of color are passionate about unity, but they recognize all too well the pain of racism in the United States and beyond. They have seen and studied the church's complicity through the centuries in crafting the abusive dynamics of racism, and they experience the continued negligence of Christians in uprooting racism and its ills in our society. The abuses of the past have been covered up, the abuses of the present continue and are explained away, the wrongs have not been righted. A call for unity could become an abusive call for abused people to drop their concerns and ignore the ongoing hurts to pretend we are "one." This is unacceptable and not a true reflection of the kingdom of God coming to earth as it is in heaven. For this reason, when I beat the drum for unity, I am simultaneously beating the drum for equity and justice in order to honor God, love my neighbor, and achieve Christ's dream of unity.

The Great Divide

Beyond ethnic division, is there any line within the Christian church which divides us more than the Catholic-Protestant chasm? Are there any two groups within Christianity who have, through the years, been less willing to learn from and partner with the other?

One of the most encouraging things within the Alpha movement has been the willingness of Catholics and Protestants to come together and run Alpha courses in order to see more people follow Jesus. It's a partnership that has been beautiful and fruitful in so many ways.

One of those responsible on the Catholic side of this partnership is Father Peter Wojcik, the director of the department of vitality and mission at the Archdiocese of Chicago. He often talks about their shift into this partnership, and how it becomes not only possible but even positive when unity, and not uniformity, is the goal.

"There is a depth of the Catholic tradition that Protestant churches can tap into," he said, "and there is a freshness of evangelicalism and the way in which we speak about faith that the Catholic church in the western world can learn from Protestant churches."

Father Peter admits that challenges always ensue when

Catholics and Protestants try to work together, but he rightly questions our motives: Do we want things *from* people or do we want things *for* people? If the goal is to make people more like me, if my primary desire is selfish, then unity and collaboration aren't possible, but if my desire is for other people to grow closer to Christ, to walk their particular path to finding him, then good things will grow out of that.

As Father Peter sees it, there are three main things we can do to lay the groundwork for this kind of unity:

Preparation. When a number of priests and lay people from the Catholic archdiocese attended the Alpha leadership conference, they took some time to prepare their people for the kinds of worship they could expect to see. When they arrived, they found people praising God through contemporary worship, which included raising their hands. The Catholic contingent wasn't used to this, but because they had talked about it beforehand, it helped them to go in and not feel uncomfortable.

Remind yourself you need to go back to God. At the end of the day, our evangelism cannot be about a certain denomination. We need to remember that it's all about leading people to Jesus Christ.

Build bridges of connection. One thing Father Peter and his group did was to help build links between their expression of faith and that of the people they would be working with. Once they saw the connections they shared within the Christian religion, they got excited, found new meaning in their own practices, and were able to identify the fears they had about each other.

The fear is there because we don't know each other. Fear removed makes room for trust and brotherhood and relationship. And once we move away from fear, we can begin to experience a sense of belonging with each other.

It's been helpful for me, as someone from a non-Catholic background, to realize I don't need to solve all the division to work together in evangelism. As my Catholic friends and I are open to working together to draw others into a growing relationship with Christ, we can come together with this gospel focus. Much like Billy Graham's approach, if there is a common passion to reach people for Christ through sharing the gospel, we can (and do) partner in such opportunities. Those are the ties that bind."

Unity, not uniformity.

Where Do We Begin?

Church United had successfully served its community of Fort Lauderdale during the hardest of times—the shooting at the Fort Lauderdale airport followed by Hurricane Irma. They had gained the city's attention and goodwill, and the unified churches felt invigorated, motivated, and excited about what they could do in the community. There was a palpable sense of goodwill between the government agencies and Church United. It felt like they were making headway.

And then another unimaginable tragedy.

A teen gunman walked into Marjory Stoneman Douglas High School in Parkland, Florida. You probably

173

remember the day. He wore a backpack loaded with ammo magazines and a black duffel bag that contained an AR-15 semi-automatic rifle. Because of this student's prior record, when a staff member saw him approaching, he issued a "Code Red" to lock down the school. But it was too late.

In less than four minutes, the shooter killed 17 people and wounded 17 more.[2]

The community, and the nation, was devastated.

Within a few hours, the school's superintendent reached out directly to Eddie. The school's leadership wanted Church United to organize the prayer vigil and community response. Less than 24 hours later, they had rallied the partner churches in the area, conducted a prayer vigil, and communicated to everyone involved that they wanted to be there for them, not just that day or that week or even that month, but for the long haul.

This started an ongoing relationship between Church United and Stoneman Douglas, a partnership that was able to raise over $200,000. Church United, to this day, is still paying for support services and counseling for those impacted by the shooting, and they completed a $95,000 upgrade of the school's landscaping to reshape the physical environment for the students as they continued going back to the same facility where the shooting took place.

"When people get a taste of what it looks like to be part of the kingdom of God outside of their church's individual brand, they come alive," Eddie told me recently. "This is what it means to be a Christian, and it necessitates a movement of the people in the pews. It can't just be the pastor doing it. Every committed Christ follower has a pen in their hand and is part of the story God is writing—that's what awakens God's people . . . Being part of God's united kingdom in south Florida isn't just about volunteering at my church on a Sunday or going to small group. We have to be part of a bigger, unified picture."

What Eddie has discovered in the five years he has led Church United is that people are starving for this kind of unified community involvement. And after they experience its sweetness, most people are legitimately confused as to why this kind of unity didn't happen earlier.

Church United's work doesn't just begin and end with providing good will to the community from churches and Christians very different from one another. It extends into evangelism. Because these churches are linked arm in arm and heart to heart, collectively their goal is to transform the entire demographic of their area. They are working and praying to see the 3 percent of Christ followers in their county transform to 6 percent over just the next few years. That's a doubling of the number of people saying yes to Jesus. It would be more than difficult for a single church to set this goal for a high-density county—but, they are not a single church, they are a unified church.

That's where Alpha came in; now we too are working with Church United to start Alpha groups in every church in their region, in addition to the students at Marjory Stoneman Douglas High School. So, collectively they can make invitations for people to come to the table of Christ, to be heard and to experience the power of God. And it's working. We've even been able to see hundreds of adults and teenagers participating in various churches near Fort Lauderdale and extending into Parkland, hungering for more, processing their hurt, and discovering Christ.

This is an unstoppable combination: demonstration of the gospel through unity, good works, and supernatural provision; space for conversation for people to belong and grow toward belief; along with proclamation of the hope of Christ to desperate hearts.

Demonstration + Conversation + Proclamation . . . that's a powerful gospel combination.

Maybe this sounds compelling to you. Maybe you find the work of Church United in South Florida and Dr. Spencer in Memphis inspiring. What are some steps you could take to explore unity with the churches in your area? Where do you even begin?

The first place to start is with repentance. "Ask the Lord . . . how your church has quietly competed with the other churches in your community, or turned a blind eye to the needs of equity and justice within minority communities, or how you may have quietly judged other Christians," Eddie suggests. "Whether you were doing it out of insecurity or fear or ignorance or a sense of self-righteousness or whatever, the first place to start is with repenting of how you may have contributed to disunity."

After that, work on getting a group of leaders together and begin by confessing that you haven't been there for the other Christians and churches represented. You haven't prayed for those churches. And if you are not in church leadership you can begin to do this work alone and with other friends in your area. Begin to ask the question, "What would it look like to see faith, hope, and love spread throughout your region? How could we make our town look more like God's kingdom on earth?" And as you do this, you'll return to the realization that this is not something you can do on your own. You will need other churches, other pastors, other congregations, other denominations, other Christians from across the way in order to make this new vision happen.

As these meetings and conversations progress, elevate the dialogue beyond your own church and start thinking about the capital-C Church—what if the churches in your city or county could be known more by what they're for than what they're against? What is a low-hanging pain point that your group of churches or a collective of unbounded Christian friendships could respond to? How could you partner with the city to alleviate this pain? You don't want to start here with a ridiculously large or obscure goal—don't begin with the goal of completely eliminating racism in your city by next week or paying for all graduating seniors' college tuition. Those are worthy goals, yes, but start with something small, something attainable, and the more wins you have, the more momentum will build.

Then, as Eddie says, "Reverse engineer unity." Start with that vision of unity in mind and pray for it together, even if it doesn't exist yet. Be what you want to see. Continue to repent together, and to each other. Ask God to birth something larger in the city. Unity is hard—you will mess up! There will be good moments and hard moments of disagreement, because you're dealing with egos and logos and sin. Type-A personality pastors and entrenched-in-their-own-ways Christians, of which there are usually many in a city or a region, will have to check some proverbial baggage at the door. Fear and insecurity, racism and judgment will creep out into the open. In spite of all this, keep praying together, keep repenting, keep working together.

Continue finding a way forward on mission together. Serve the needs of your city as we've discussed. But don't stop there. Extend the unity effort into evangelism by trying something such as Alpha (or another evangelism effort) together. Eddie maintains, "Alpha is such an easy way to help lay people recognize that they are part of a bigger picture . . . Alpha allows the other 96 percent—those not gifted in evangelism—to come together to reach the lost in their community." As you invite people to Alpha, you invite them into this greater movement of service and love in the community, and it can be one of the leading tools of evangelism in your congregation.

Eddie shared a story with me about a guy who came to faith in Alpha at one of the churches who was part of Church United. When he heard about the work they were doing with all these other churches, he got excited about it—he wanted to see his neighbors come to faith, and this work of unity inspired him. So, he reached out to Eddie and said, "Look, I've got a lucrative construction company that basically prints money. I'm an ATM machine. Seriously. I have been so impacted by Alpha and the fact that all of these churches are uniting, I'd like to be a patron and an investor in this kind of evangelistic work of unity." Now, he funds the Church United effort and the expansion of Alpha.

"His involvement in our work never would have happened if we weren't building unity and running Alpha, because Alpha not only bridges the divide for non-Christians to Christ, it also bridges the divide among churches within a city. If Alpha and Church United are able to connect the broader, capital-C Church together in unity around the gospel of Jesus Christ. That's what excites him."

Finally, Eddie has discovered a kind of secret sauce that has held their work at Church United together—invest in pastors, and work to create a safe third space for them. This allows pastors who previously might have seen each other as competition to come together, to realize that these other pastors are just like them, and to explore what it might look like to trust God together.

Our greatest apologetic, according to Eddie *and* Jesus, is the way we work together in our communities.

What would it look like for you to begin talking about unity among the churches in your community? What would it look like for you to pursue unity with other Jesus followers from different Christ-centered faith and ethnic backgrounds in your city?

Remember the words from John 17:22–23:

"I have given them the glory that you gave me, that they may be one as we are one—I in them and you in me—so that they may be brought to complete unity. Then the world will know that you sent me and have loved them even as you have loved me."

"Complete unity . . . then the world will know."
Are you and I willing to pursue unity, together, so that the world may know?

What Next?

- What steps have you and your church already taken toward unity, not just uniformity?
- What is challenging for you about bridging historical lines of division within the Christian tradition?
- What new steps are you openly taking toward a church of another ethnic background and Christ-centered denominational tradition?
- Consider someone in your community—someone from another *tribe*—whom you can begin taking steps toward unity.

One More Time

Two weeks before Thanksgiving, I had a dream about my uncle. It was one of those engages-all-your-senses dreams—the kind of dream that feels so real, when you wake up, you can't shake it. I'm not normally a dream guy who tries to interpret what happened and why, but when I woke up, I knew it was significant.

I should tell you that at that point I hadn't spoken with my uncle in about two years. Some background: when he was a teenager, the cops knocked on the door of his home every two weeks or so, wondering where he was and if he was connected to whatever recent questionable activity had taken place in town. From there, he was sent to military school. He got married, had children, and then, over the years, lost the relationships with his wife and children to the results of poor choices, hard living, family fights, and all the rest you can imagine. Over time, he became almost entirely estranged from them and the rest of our extended family.

I spent 20 years building a relationship with him as best as I could. We did a few construction projects together, and even though there was a lot of internal family conflict which he was involved in, I spent hours listening to him gradually share about his life and the challenges he had faced. Occasionally we talked about spiritual things, and I invited him to church and gave him books to hopefully draw him closer to Christ. I shared the hope of Jesus with him for many years, but he was like a stubborn brick wall and never moved an inch.

For him, there was no God and no reason for God. He was truly a materialist and a humanist—there was nothing in the universe beyond what he could see with his two eyes and touch with his hands.

In the dream, I had been building a house with my uncle, just the two of us, and as I emerged up out of the dream I had this sense that God was saying, "I want to build something beautiful together." This message hounded me all morning, right up until I opened my Bible for my daily reading, which happened to be Ezekiel 33:1–6:

> The word of the LORD came to me: "Son of man, speak to your people . . . blow[s] the trumpet to warn the people, then if anyone hears the trumpet but does not heed the warning . . . their blood will be on their own head . . . But if the watchman sees the sword coming and does not blow the trumpet to warn the people . . . that person's life will be taken because of their sin, but I will hold the watchman accountable for their blood."

Well, those are harsh words, but they are from the Word of God. Combined with the dream I'd had about my uncle, and these new words, an urgency burst into my mind. I needed to speak with my uncle about his salvation, right away. I needed to blow the trumpet. And then I read verse seven:

> . . . "Son of man, I have made you a watchman for the people of Israel; so hear the word I speak and give them warning from me."

I get the picture, God.

The thing was, I hadn't talked to my uncle for such a long time that I had given up hope on his ever coming around to believing the gospel and trusting Christ. I knew he had smoked a few packs of Lucky Strike (filter-less) cigarettes a day. I knew he had recently been diagnosed with lung cancer, and I later found out he had had a heart attack, but the doctors couldn't operate because of his overall health. I felt so hopeless, and I didn't want to go through the same humiliation again of bringing up God and him dismissing me out of hand.

But the still and not-so small voice in my soul wouldn't let me off the hook. It was like that first passage we talked about, the one in Luke 5, had been written just for me.

> When he had finished speaking, he said to Simon, "Put out into deep water, and let down the nets for a catch."

183

Simon answered, "Master, we've worked hard all night and haven't caught anything. But because you say so, I will let down the nets."

Let out your net again, Craig. I know you've tried before. I know you've worked hard all night and haven't caught any-thing. Try one more time.

"Because you say so," was my response. "Because you say so, I'll try one more time."

So, I called my uncle to see if I could come visit him, then looked at my calendar and realized I already had a trip to his area (on the other side of the country) scheduled about a week from that time. We agreed on a good time for me to visit, and soon after that I found myself knocking on his door.

I wasn't prepared for the man who answered. He looked close to death. He was pale and bony, and he couldn't walk six steps across the room without stopping for a minute, leaning against whatever he could find, and catching his breath. He wheeled his oxygen tank along behind. I looked at him and thought about the hard life he had lived, and I was filled with such compassion and some confusion for the long road he had traveled.

I helped him go through a few end-of-life legal documents and witnessed his signature on some others. We discussed his power of attorney, his will, and such. For a while I was mostly quiet, just listening, because I had tried to talk about God with him so many times before, and he had been so hardened for so many years.

But I decided I needed to tell him the story of my dad.

"You know, John," I began, "I was with my dad not long before he died, and I was doing these very things for him. We were setting up his power of attorney, and I told him, 'Dad, it's time to set up a power of attorney for your soul. You've never made peace with God on your own or found forgiveness or wholeness, and the only person who can do that for you is Jesus. If you hand over leadership of your life to him, he will establish for you peace with the Lord forever.' Would you like to do that, just like my dad did?"

My uncle just sat there, listening, his breathing coming in clicks through the tube that went under his nose from the oxygen tank.

I said it again. "He did it, John. My dad who stiff-armed God for 74 years signed over power of attorney for his soul to Jesus. It's your turn now."

I waited. Here was this guy who for years had shut down every spiritual conversation I had ever brought up for decades. I was so nervous.

"You know the end is coming soon," I continued. "You can be at peace with Jesus now and forever. You can be free of all the wrongs of life if you would only give your heart to him right now. Would you do that?"

I practically held my breath. I could hear him exhale. Inhale.

"Yes," he said in a quiet voice. "I would love to do that right now."

"Okay," I said, and to be honest, I was completely stunned, I didn't think I'd ever see this moment. "Let's pray."

I have to confess, when I drove up to his house that day, I hardly had even a tiny amount of faith he would accept Jesus. Maybe just a mustard seed of faith. I remember thinking during the whole trip, off and on, *What am I doing? This is not going to work. It's only going to make him angry and push him further away in these final moments.*

Yet, there I was, leading him through a prayer to accept Christ. After we finished praying, I could feel myself tearing up. He looked at me with this sort of contented grin.

"Craig," he said, "don't you think I'm about to shed a tear now too."

"Well, I am," I replied. "And I will." And we laughed together.

I sat there in that moment, and the sound of my own voice felt far away. I had cast my net into the deeper waters on the other side of the boat, and Jesus' way had worked.

"You can know," I continued. "You can know right now, you can pass on in peace. You belong to the Lord. He fills you now and forever with his Spirit."

I paused.

"I love you, Uncle John."

"I love you too, Craig."

He had never said that to me before in my life. And before I left, we hugged, something else we had never done before. As I drove away, I thought of the simplicity of the thief hanging next to Jesus on his own cross. It was a poignant moment of crying out in desperation to Christ, and his life and death were forever changed. Eternity split in two for that man's life and now for my uncle as well.

How to Begin Following Jesus

At some point in the journey of sharing our faith we have to move a step further than all we've discussed in this book:

When we've hungered for more,
when we've created space for conversation,
when we've built a sense of belonging,
when we've introduced people to an experience,
    not just an explanation,
when we've showed the fruit of our faith and not
    just the facts,
when we've mobilized we not just me,
when we've sought unity, not just uniformity . . .

When the Holy spirit says "NOW," then we need to be able to clearly share the gospel of Christ. There comes a time when proclamation is necessary, when we must state the truth of Jesus and invite people to make a decision to follow him, just as I did with my uncle.

Here's how I often do it (this comes from the appendix in my book, *How to Follow Jesus*[1]). I begin by sharing John 1:12:

Yet to all who did receive him, to those who believed in his name, he gave the right to become children of God.

And then I say something like, "Beginning a relationship with Jesus is being adopted into the family of God. God is always, actively drawing us back to himself. He is the good Father working to bring those who feel far from him back into his family, back to his table of forgiveness and fulfillment."

Receiving Jesus is the starting line of a lifelong faith. If you feel stuck—somewhat empty or confused about whether you are his—it only requires a decision and a genuine prayer of your heart. Maybe it's time to take the words of John 1:12 as your own: "Receive him . . . believe in his name . . . and become a child of God."

After that, I walk people through the simple, *I'm Sorry–Thank You–Please* prayer. It's a clear and simple prayer where we say, "I'm sorry, thank you, and please," like having a conversation with a dad we've walked out on.

> **I'm sorry**, God, I've turned away from you and your ways all this time. I've done wrong and now I want that to end. I want to be yours. I choose for you to begin leading my life.
>
> **Thank you**, Jesus, for dying on the cross. You paid the price for the wrongs I've done and taken my place. You have forgiven me. You rose from the dead so that, in you, I can rise from my death and separation from God now and for eternity.
>
> **Please**, Holy Spirit, come and fill me. I'm open to be led by you forever. I commit my life to you now, in Jesus' name.

It may be a short prayer, but history splits in two whenever it is said. From this moment on, the person who prays it is his. Nothing can ever change that. The moment can't be undone by living imperfectly; it can't be improved upon by achieving perfection. The person who prays the prayer is his, a child of God.

That's it. We have the words of truth and when the soil is tilled, people say "Yes!" again and again. What is more fulfilling than being a conduit of God's heavenly kingdom coming to earth in this way?

That amazing trip I took to visit my uncle was just before Thanksgiving. On New Year's Eve day, I received a call from a number I didn't recognize. It was from the hospital to which my uncle had been recently rushed. It was time to take him off life support. They just thought I should know.

They did remove him from the ventilator, and he died 30 minutes later.

It was two and a half months since I had the dream. Had I not trusted the Holy Spirit and stepped forward, following Jesus' way, had I not been willing to once again sail out into deep water, well, who knows?

And it wasn't just that one moment with him that allowed me to share the gospel. It was years of listening, years of trust-building and belonging, years of a fruit-filled faith, and years of shared meals and conversations.

Who knows? But now, he's free.

Praise the Lord.

For his presence and heart.

For his grace to wipe the slate clean.

For his grace to give me a prophetic dream in the
moment when I needed it.
For his grace to give me the stern warning from
Ezekiel when I woke up.
For his grace to go with me again into deep water.

Will you do it again? Will you put all previous attempts that ended up looking like failure behind you and row out into deep water, let out your nets one more time?

Will you try to reach those you love, acquaintances in your life, and your surrounding community again, but this time doing it Jesus' way?

If you'll do it, there is an entire group of people waiting for you whose lives could be transformed. An entire catch you never could have dreamed of, one you will not be able to pull in on your own.

Revive evangelism, together, with me.

Let's do it Jesus' way.

What Next?

- Who in your life does not know Jesus that God is trying to get your attention about?
- What does "putting out your nets one more time" on behalf of that person look like?
- Try to memorize and role play in your own words the framework from John 1:12 (Believe + Receive = Become) and the "I'm Sorry, Thank You, Please" prayer model so you are ready for when the time comes.
- Cry out to God in lengthy prayer for the sake of this person.

Notes

Introduction

1. *Reviving Evangelism* (Barna Group, 2019), 10.
2. Ibid., 11.
3. Ibid., 10.
4. *The Great Opportunity* (Pinetops Foundation, 2018), 9.
5. https://www.pewforum.org/2019/10/17/in-u-s-decline -of-christianity-continues-at-rapid-pace/.
6. *The Great Opportunity*, 33.
7. *Reviving Evangelism*, 47.
8. Ibid.
9. *Reviving Evangelism*, 68.
10. Ibid.
11. Ibid.
12. Kinnaman, David. *Faith for Exiles* (Grand Rapids: Baker Books, 2019).
13. "Parenting in America." Pew Research Center (blog). Dec. 17, 2015. https://www.pewsocialtrends.org /2015/12/17/1-the-american-family-today/.
14. Mammoser, Gigen. "The FOMO Is Real: How Social Media Increases Depression and Loneliness." *Healthline*

(blog). Dec. 9, 2018. https://www.healthline.com
/health-news/social-media-use-increases-depression
-and-loneliness#Does-social-media-cause-depression?

Chapter 1: Hungry for More, Not Just Hoping for Many

1. *Reviving Evangelism*, 73.
2. Ibid.
3. Jon Tyson tells the story of this trip and how each of the locations impacted him in a sermon. Church of the City. "Teach Us to Pray: Prayer for Spiritual Awakening." YouTube video. Aug. 27, 2018, https://www.youtube.com/watch?v=AdtrvBHQQvM.
4. The Works of Jonathan Edwards, *Vol. 4: The Great Awakening*, ed. C. C. Goen (New Haven, CT: Yale University Press, 1972), 21.
5. Jon Tyson, "Teach Us to Pray."
6. I compiled these steps after a conversation with Jon Tyson about revival. These are five things Jon recommends if you have a desire for personal revival.

Chapter 2: Conversation, Not Just Proclamation

1. This story was told to me by Drew Hyun, the founding pastor of Hope Church New York City. I am indebted to him and his work for many of the thoughts I share in this chapter.
2. Copenhaver, Martin B. *Jesus Is the Question* (Nashville: Abingdon Press, 2014).

3. *Reviving Evangelism*, 54.

4. Ibid.

5. Zender, Jack, and Joseph Folkman, "What Great Listeners Actually Do," *Harvard Business Review*, July, 2016. https://hbr.org/2016/07/what-great-listeners-actually-do.

6. Zenger and Folkman, "What Great Listeners Actually Do."

7. Augsburger, David. *Caring Enough to Hear and Be Heard* (Ventura, CA: Regal Books, 1982), 12.

8. Zenger and Folkman, "What Great Listeners Actually Do."

9. Hybels, Bill and Mark Mittelberg. *Becoming a Contagious Christian* (Grand Rapids: Zondervan, 1996).

Chapter 3: Belonging, Not Just Welcoming

1. https://www.merriam-webster.com/dictionary/host.

2. *Reviving Evangelism*, 80.

3. https://tnjn.com/2014/05/17/tnjn-spotlight-star bucks-creates-sense-of-belonging-for-customers/.

4. Alton, Larry. "The Five Emotions that Drive Customer Loyalty." *Entrepreneur*, August 4, 2016. *https://www.entrepreneur.com/article/280254*.

5. *Reviving Evangelism*, 10.

6. Ibid.

7. I am indebted to a recent conversation with my friend Glenn Packiam in which he talked about these four ways to begin practicing radical hospitality. For a beautiful unpacking of this concept, please read his book, *Blessed, Broken, Given*.

Chapter 4: Experience, Not Just Explanation

1. https://www.vineyardchurches.org.uk/about/john
-wimber/.
2. *Reviving Evangelism*, 56.
3. These ideas came out of a conversation I had with
my friend Jay Pathak, pastor of Mile High Vineyard.
Check out his book, *The Art of Neighboring*.

Chapter 5: Fruitful, Not Just Factual

1. Kevin shared this story at a recent Outreach
conference. I highly recommend his book, *Unlikely*,
in which he shares this story, and some of the
concepts I'm writing about, in greater detail.
2. *Reviving Evangelism*, 54.
3. Ibid., 71.
4. Ibid., 56.

Chapter 6: We, Not Just Me

1. https://www.barna.com/research/survey-describes
-the-spiritual-gifts-that-christians-say-they-have/.

Chapter 7: Unity, Not Just Uniformity

1. *Reviving Evangelism*, 56.
2. https://www.history.com/this-day-in-history/park
land-marjory-stoneman-douglas-school-shooting.

Conclusion

1. Springer, Craig. *How to Follow Jesus: A Practical Guide
for Growing Your Faith* (Grand Rapids: Zondervan,
2020), appendix.

What is Alpha?

Alpha is a conversation series designed for people to explore the meaning of life, the Christian faith, ask questions, and share their point of view. Everyone is welcome. Alpha is run all around the globe in online groups, cafés, churches, universities, homes, prisons—you name it. No two Alphas look exactly the same, but generally they have three key elements in common: connect with others, watch a short film, and discuss your thoughts.

Ready to get started?

Visit **www.alphausa.org/getstarted** to find free, helpful training tools and practical next steps to launch your own Alpha group. We always give Alpha away for free!

How to Follow Jesus

Millior
but do   **DATE DUE**
Christians, new believers often end
up paralyzed. They become overwhelmed trying to master complicated
doctrines, frustrated by a large list of
rules for policing their lives, and be-
wildered by a new (and strange) vo-
cabulary. Even worse, there are few
books offering simple and clear advice to guide a Christian's
first spiritual steps that are written in common, contemporary
language. Until now.

In *How to Follow Jesus*, Craig Springer, executive director of
Alpha USA, one of America's most effective evangelism movements, explodes numerous myths surrounding the Christian
faith that create unnecessary obstacles to growth, including: il-
lustrating that sin and temptation are not the greatest threat to
a flourishing faith; forgiveness means going through rather than
around our feelings; and how disappointment in the church may
be the essential step in growing a foundation for life-changing
community. Sharing personal stories from his own journey to a
mature faith, Springer sets readers at ease and offers them practical, easy-to-implement advice for following Jesus. Destined to
become a timeless classic, *How to Follow Jesus* is a must read
for new and returning Christians.

Available in stores and online!